The Richmon

The ministers at St Mary Magdalene
and their role in the community

Derek Robinson

The Museum of Richmond

Foreword

Whenever we talk about a church it is easy to think merely of a building and St Mary Magdalene, which has evolved over the centuries and is still at the heart of Richmond, is indeed a beautiful and much loved building.

However, church in its truest sense is about people – those who worship there or take part in its life. Over the centuries many have come for baptisms or weddings, for funeral services, for regular services or simply to find a moment's peace in a busy world. The people who form the church include those who are appointed as vicars of the Church of St Mary Magdalene. Under their servant leadership each of the vicars will have brought (and bring) their own style to the vocation that is ministry and will have shaped the life of the church in Richmond as well as its interaction with the local community.

Derek Robinson has researched the lives of those who have been vicars at St Mary Magdalene with great enthusiasm and written their stories with skill. He has unearthed details forgotten in time and brought them back for us to smile about, to reflect upon and to inspire us. We are indebted to him for enhancing our celebrations of the history of this Christian place of worship.

Revd Wilma Roest

Vicar St Mary Magdalene
Team Rector Richmond Team Ministry

July 2019

Acknowledgements

It is unlikely that this book would have ever been conceived, let alone written, were it not for A. Cecil Piper. Piper, a worshipper at St Mary Magdalene and for many years the Borough Librarian of Richmond, published his book *A History of the Parish Church of St Mary Magdalene, Richmond, Surrey* in 1947, the outcome of years of research. It still remains the most comprehensive history of the church although, as regards past vicars, he felt it fitting to proceed no further than the end of the eighteenth century.

A big debt of gratitude is also owed to the late John Cloake, whose research on the ministers of St Mary Magdalene before 1660, the locations in Richmond of past vicarages, the pulpit, and the history of the Queen's Road development all proved invaluable (see Further Reading). Also, his Magnum Opus, *Cottages and Common Fields of Richmond and Kew*, the fruit of forty years work into the history of Richmond and Kew, provided much additional useful information.

I am particularly grateful to John Oates, Bruce Carpenter, Julian Reindorp, Robert Titley and Wilma Roest for the great trouble each of them took in providing me with biographical detail. Thanks are also due to Donatella Astratti, Peter Bowyer, Valerie Boyes, Cynthia Hill, Rebecca Phelps and Paul Velluet for their help on a number of research topics. And, finally, many thanks to the helpful staff at Richmond Local Studies Library and Archive.

This book has been supported by generous individual donors, the Richmond Church Charity Estates and the National Lottery through the National Lottery Heritage Fund.

Richmond Church Charity Estates

Front cover image and right:
Thomas Wakefield vicar 1776–1806

Text © Derek Robinson, 2019
Published by The Museum of Richmond, August 2019
Designed by Jackie Baines Studio
Printed by Pulsar Print Management Ltd
Set in 10pt Frutiger 45 light and Frutiger 55
ISBN 978-0-9518549-2-1

CONTENTS

Introduction

As with all very long-established churches St Mary Magdalene, historically the parish church of Richmond, has seen many vicars come and go over the centuries. The stories to be told of these individuals, and their periods of incumbency, reflect their various and differing personalities and the times they lived through; they also capture, to some extent, the life of St Mary Magdalene since its early beginnings.

This book seeks to bring alive again the vicars of Richmond from past centuries, and to celebrate those still with us. Although information about ministers from the earlier years is a little thin, the hope is that most ministers from the seventeenth century onwards have been provided with sufficiently rounded portraits to give a feel for both who they were and their time at St Mary Magdalene. These portraits, it should be said, are sketches rather than exhaustive biographies; to have attempted the latter would have been to test both the patience of the reader and the ability of the author.

The book begins, necessarily, with discussion of the date of St Mary Magdalene, its relationship in earlier centuries to what was then its mother church, All Saints, Kingston, and other explanatory material. However, readers need not feel inhibited should they wish to start by dipping into the biographies of the vicars; those of the nineteenth century are the author's particular favourite.

It is important to remember that the stories which have come down to us give but only a fleeting view of the ongoing, daily life of a vicar; a life of ministering to parishioners, and of prayer and preaching. As Canon George Gray (1928–46) said when the time came for him to move on to another parish, 'the work of a vicar is continuous'. Nor have vicars ever acted alone, being supported by curates, church wardens and, particularly in more recent years, their spouses.

It should perhaps also be emphasised that this book focuses upon the lives of the ministers in charge at what, historically, has been the parish church, St Mary Magdalene. To have added biographies of the very many curates who have worked in the parish, and of the vicars in more recent times at the two sister churches of St John the Divine and St Matthias, would have considerably widened both the scope and purpose of the book.

One common thread running through these stories is the notable fact that of the nine vicars between 1696 and 1900 all but one, Thomas Young (1806–17), died whilst still in office at Richmond. Would it be too fanciful to conclude that, once appointed, all these vicars very quickly came to realise that they had most definitely landed on their feet!

The date of St Mary Magdalene

Identifying the date on which a church was first established in Richmond has proved a frustrating exercise. The earliest documentary evidence of the existence of a church is contained in the records of Merton Priory of 1211:

> 'To the parish church of Kingston-upon-Thames, Surrey, which from a very early date had been appropriated to the Priory, there were attached four chapelries, viz., Ditton, East Moulsey, Ham or Petersham, and Shene, each of which had an endowment'

Merton Priory was founded in 1114, and one possible interpretation of the above is that Shene chapelry – Shene was renamed Richmond in 1501 – was already in existence and transferred to the Priory shortly after 1114, implying that a church was established in Richmond more than nine hundred years ago. It is improbable, although not impossible, that it was established even earlier since, unlike the nearby church in Petersham, there is no mention of Shene chapel in the Domesday Book (which was completed in 1086). What is clear is that a chapel was in existence some time before 1211, but that the date on which it was first established remains a matter for speculation. The best guess is that a chapel will initially have been founded in Richmond in the twelfth century. That chapel will probably have been on the site of the present church of St Mary Magdalene but, again, there is an absence of hard facts. The earliest documentary evidence for a church on that site is contained in a will dated 1487.

The earliest surviving parts of the present church are the brick structural core in part of the tower, and the stone arched opening in the nave which date from the late fifteenth century; the flint facing with stone dressings was added early in the twentieth century.

The status of St Mary Magdalene and its ministers

Until 1852, when it finally became an independent parish, St Mary Magdalene was a chapelry to its mother church, Kingston. Whilst that can be simply stated, it is the case that over the centuries the perceived status of the church changed from time to time. For example, in the early eighteenth century the members of the Vestry, the body overseeing parochial business, seem to have convinced at least themselves that St Mary Magdalene had by then become wholly independent of Kingston.

As mentioned above, reference to the status of Richmond first occurs in the Merton Priory records of 1211 where, as Shene, it was named as a chapelry of Kingston. The structure of parishes across the country at that time, and the degree of autonomy of chapelries, was very fluid. At one extreme were chapelries wholly reliant upon a visiting minister from the mother church. At the other were chapelries with their own chaplain on a modest salary. Under the terms of an agreement made between the prior of Merton and the vicar of Kingston in 1375, Richmond was to fall within the latter category.

The purpose of the 1375 agreement was to regulate the affairs of Kingston and its four chapelries, and to resolve a dispute that had arisen between the prior and the vicar over who was liable for repair costs. By this agreement the vicar was to provide 'fit chaplains' and to arrange for the administration of the sacraments, and also to appoint fit and proper persons to be parish clerks and officers at the chapels. The prior, for his part, assigned land in each place on which the vicar of Kingston undertook to build, and maintain, a manse (vicarage) for the chaplain.

Richmond very nearly became an independent parish when, in 1658, Commissioners appointed by the Commonwealth Parliament reported that 'the said Chappelrye of Richmond, West Sheene and Kew be divided from the Vicaridge and pish of Kingston And made a distinct pish of itself devided from the Vicaridge of Kingston aforesaid…'. However, that recommendation was never acted upon, probably because most of the legislation of the Commonwealth was repealed or suspended following the restoration of the monarchy in 1660.

The independence issue was soon to resurface when, in 1679, Nicholas Hardinge, the patron of Kingston, claimed that he was entitled to certain fees and tithes (a form of tax) from Richmond. Hardinge had acquired the patronage of the living of Kingston in 1672. Eventually he withdrew his claim, accepting that the fees and tithes were perquisites of the minister and churchwardens of Richmond. The implication is that Richmond at that time had acquired a semi-autonomous status.

The matter arose again fifty years later when, in 1729, there was a dispute between the Richmond Vestry and the vicar of Kingston, Rev. William Comer. Rev. Richard Coleire had been appointed minister of Isleworth in 1716 and, in 1720, of Kingston, holding the two posts concurrently until, in 1726, he was appointed minister of Richmond, whereupon he resigned Kingston so that, as he stated in a biographical questionnaire now held at the Bodleian Library, he might 'hold Richmond with Isleworth'. Subsequently Rev. Comer commenced an action to have Rev. Coleire's licence revoked, with the apparent intention of coming to Richmond himself. The Vestry expressed outrage at the vicar of Kingston's pretentions 'to make this Parish a Chappell of Ease to Kingston', although legally that is exactly what it was. The grounds for Rev. Comer's action are unknown, but the implications are that at that time Richmond was regarded by many as independent from Kingston. Rev. Comer was supported in his action by the patron of Kingston, Nicholas Hardinge (son of the Nicholas Hardinge referred to above), so this may have been a resumption of the 1679 dispute; the patron seeking to obtain control of the fees and tithes through appointing his own man as minister at Richmond.

The outcome of this dispute was that Rev. Coleire continued as perpetual curate for Richmond, albeit after surrendering his original licence and obtaining a new one from the bishop. It seems improbable that the new licence will have been in identical terms, so perhaps Nicholas Hardinge was the victor of this dispute. The final twist in the tale of this saga is that when Rev. Coleire died, in 1746, Rev. Comer, who was then still vicar of Kingston, lost little time in securing the vacancy for himself.

The rather informal arrangements that had subsisted since the 1375 agreement were regularised in 1769 when, by an Act of Parliament, the Vicarage of Kingston and the Chapelry of Richmond, together with the hamlets of Ham and Hook, were established as a separate Vicarage, known as 'The Vicarage of Kingston-upon-Thames and Sheen otherwise Richmond'. However, Kingston continued as the mother church, and the right of nomination of the minister at Richmond lay with the vicar of Kingston. The term 'Vicarage', it should be added, did not then refer to the vicarage house; broadly speaking, it was what we now know as a parish.

Finally, by an Act of Parliament of 1849, Richmond became a separate parish, wholly independent of Kingston. The Act took effect in 1852 following the death of Rev. Samuel Gandy, the incumbent vicar of the pre-existing parish. St Mary Magdalene was initially the only church in the parish until, in 1831, St John the Divine was built as a chapel of ease to the parish church. That relationship was short-lived however since, in 1838, a new parish was formed with St John the Divine as its parish church. In 1858 the church of St Matthias was built as another chapel of ease to St Mary Magdalene, to accommodate the growing population of Richmond. And in 1976 the church of St John the Divine was reunited with the parish of Richmond. In 1996 the three churches became the members of Richmond Team Ministry.

Although the status of the church of St Mary Magdalene, and that of its ministers, has shifted over the centuries, there is one important legacy of the 1375 agreement that is still very much with us. The charity, Richmond Church Charity Estates, which provides significant financial support to the parish and which almost wholly funded the recent major works on the fabric of St Mary Magdalene, is thought to have originated from the Merton Priory endowment of 1375. If that is correct, the charity is one of the oldest registered charities in the country.

Patrons and advowsons

The present patron of St Mary Magdalene is King's College, Cambridge. Its role is now limited to voting on the appointment of a Team Rector to Richmond Team Ministry, but historically patronage provided the holder with wider powers and some financial benefits. The right to appoint a priest – known as an advowson – was capable of being bought and sold as an investment, the price varying according to the value of the living and the condition of the parsonage.

As mentioned above, the Hardinge family owned the advowson for the living of Kingston, Richmond's mother church, in the seventeenth and eighteenth centuries, and were involved in legal actions regarding their rights, possibly with a view to securing a financial benefit. The patronage passed down the family to George Hardinge who sold it, in 1786, to the Provost and Fellows of King's College, Cambridge.

Vicars, curates and ministers

The word 'curate' is today generally taken to mean a priest in their first office post-ordination, but this usage is quite recent. In the 1662 Prayer Book the term had the meaning of the incumbent of a benefice, the person licensed by the bishop for the 'cure of souls' within a benefice. Depending upon the structure of the benefice a curate was either a rector, a vicar or a perpetual curate. However, in practice the word 'curate' was often given a wider meaning, and an assistant given substantial responsibility for one of the churches within a benefice might be referred to as the curate in charge. 'Benefice' is not easily defined but, broadly speaking, equates to a 'parish'.

In the records relating to St Mary Magdalene, the terms vicar, rector, canon, chaplain, curate, perpetual curate, and minister are all used at various times when referring to the parish priest. The description normally used until late in the sixteenth century was 'curate', and then 'minister' until, in 1852, Richmond became a separate parish and the parish priest became the 'vicar'. When the Team Ministry was created in 1996 the vicar became the Team Rector. 'Canon' is usually an honorary title conferred upon senior parish priests who have provided long and dedicated service to the diocese.

In the nineteenth and twentieth centuries the vicar often had four, sometimes even five, curates supporting his work in the parish – preaching, ministering to the sick, holding Bible classes and so on. Often these were young men, fresh from university, and from time to time they overstepped the mark. Earnest, intense Evangelicals were to cause headaches for both Rev. Gandy and Rev. Procter.

Ministers in the early years

Under the terms of the agreement of 1375 it fell to the vicar of Kingston to appoint 'fit chaplains' to the Shene chapelry (see p.3). The arrangements applying prior to this are unknown but the manorial roll of the manor of Shene in 1314, in addition to providing a fascinating picture of Richmond in the fourteenth century and the types of work its inhabitants then did, may possibly include the first name we have for an acting minister. The village is estimated to have consisted of little more than forty cottages, mostly grouped along the south-east side of the Green, but a few others along the road (now George Street) north of the church. Included in the roll are the names of John le Clerke and William atte Churche, both freemen, and it is possible that one of these may have been the priest, the other his sexton.

The earliest formal records of the names of ministers date from 1614 when the Richmond Select Vestry was established. However, in the course of his extensive researches into the history of Richmond, John Cloake found a number of references to incumbents who were named in the wills of Richmond residents or in other documents. The fruits of his research were published in an article in *Richmond History No.14*, 'Curates and Ministers of Richmond Parish Church before 1660', which includes a list of all the incumbents he had identified. Those ministers appointed prior to the seventeenth century, and the dates on which their names occur, in wills and other documents, are listed below. Most of these incumbents will have served for a number of years, spanning the dates on which their names were recorded.

William Hyne	1487
Robert Dawell	1514
John Terne	1517–21
Nicholas Rycords	1522
William -	1525
William Wylson	1541
Christopher Downbanke	1549
James Norris	1555
James Johnson	1557
James Man	1569–74
John Skeat	1580
Ithall Griffyth	1597–99
Thomas Browne	1601

There is a stone tablet by the West door of St Mary Magdalene, which includes some, but not all of the above, namely Wylson, Downbanke, Norris, Skeat and Browne. Thomas Browne's date is there given as 1596 which, as Cloake notes, appears to be in error given that he succeeded Ithall Griffyth as incumbent. Browne died in an epidemic which struck Richmond in 1603. The tablet also includes the name of Walter Rogers with the date 1586. He was in fact minister of Petersham, and it seems doubtful if he was ever appointed to Richmond.

The first minister at Shene to have been identified is 'Sir' William Hyne who died in 1487. Until the mid-sixteenth century 'Sir' was commonly used as a courtesy title for a priest. The terms of his will, made on 17 July 1487, were as follows:

> To be buried in the church of St Mary Magdalene, Shene, before the high altar there. To my mother one sheep. To the light of St Mary, Shene 2 sheep. To the light of St Mary Magdalene 5 sheep. For the building of the steeple of the same church 20s. To William Gardiner

2 sheep. To William Symball 2 sheep. To each of my godsons 2 sheep. To my mother 40s. To Margaret Makareth my best gown with a hood. Residue to Sir William Cardmaker, Vicar of Twykynham, Sir John Wodhous of Hampton and Sir Gilbert Story of Colbrok *Executors*, for the welfare of my soul. To a suitable priest to celebrate for my soul and the souls of all the faithful dead in the said church for one year 9 marks. To my executors 4 silver spoons. To Sir Richaard Wodehous a silver spoon.

The sheep bequeathed 'to the light' of the Virgin Mary and St Mary Magdalene were probably kept on church land and their wool sold to purchase candles to illumine images in the church of Saints Mary and Mary Magdalene. The fact that the residue of Hyne's estate was to be applied 'for the welfare of my soul', belying the dictum that 'you cannot take it with you', might raise eyebrows among present day probate lawyers.

Nicholas Rycords, who as 'Curate of Richmond' witnessed the will of Raufe Frensch on 24 December 1522, is also mentioned in court records – 'Master Nicholas, Curate of Richmond was paid 6s 8d from Princess Mary's privy purse for a wax taper offered in the princess's chapel on the feast of the Purification'. This implies that there were links at that time between the chapel at Richmond Palace and St Mary Magdalene.

Homes of the Vicars

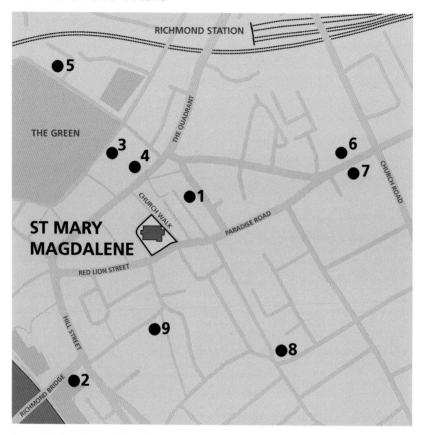

1 Probable site of 14th century manse
   Stephen Benham 1624
2 Abiel Borfet from 1683
3 Nicholas Brady from 1716
4 Richard Coleire 1729–46
5 William Comer 1749–66
   Dupuis to Gray 1852–1946
6 George Wakefield 1771–76
7 Thomas Wakefield from 1779
8 Thomas Young from 1806
9 Barlow to Roest 1946–

Some of the clergy lived in more than one house during their time at Richmond – Borfet, Brady, Coleire, and Comer. For full details, see the textrelating to each minister. The above shows those properties in which each spent the longest time.

Ministers in the 17th century

A 17th century minister

Stephen Benham: 1614–47

The first minister of whom we have some biographical detail is Stephen Benham.

Benham was the minister at Richmond when the Select Vestry was created in 1614. The Vestry, established by licence of the Bishop of Winchester, formalised the government of the parish, including the levying of a money rate for maintenance of the church and its minister, and Benham's name appears as one of its original members. It is probable, however, that he became minister before 1614. He is recorded as having been minister at Petersham 'about 1603', and appears to have held both posts concurrently until he was replaced at Petersham between 1631–34. The denouement of the Select Vestry, a century later, is discussed at p.32.

During Benham's ministry St Mary Magdalene had to be enlarged to accommodate the growing population of Richmond, and the addition of a south aisle was completed in 1617. Also, quite extensive works were carried out in 1624 on repairing the tower. At that time the church accommodated about 300 people in its pews, for which pew rents had to be paid, and there was additional free seating for the poor, school children and domestic servants. An entry in the Vestry Minutes, dated 9 October 1637, provides a nice insight into the occasionally lively behaviour of some during church services:

> Also that Symon Hues is to be paid 4d. every Lords day for the

quieting of the Children in divine Service and Whipping out of the doggs the said 4d. to be paid by the Churchwardens.

In 1644 Benham was caught up in the strife of the Civil War, and was suspended by an order made by the Committee for Plundered Ministers. Set up by the Long Parliament in 1643, the original purpose of the Committee was to provide support for plundered ministers – that is, ministers who had previously been evicted from their livings by Royalists. However, it quickly became a process for removing 'scandalous' clerics who were thought to support the monarchy, although 'scandalous' was given a wide definition – 'any minister who was non-resident, incompetent or idle, scandalous either in life or doctrine, or in any way ill-affected to Parliament'; High Anglican clerics fell within this definition, the majority of Parliament being pro-Presbyterian. The nature of Benham's alleged transgressions is unknown.

The process for suspending ministers, and taking possession of their houses, was a slow and cumbersome paper-chase, and Benham's case was no exception. He refused to quit, failed to appear before the Committee when summonsed, and forbade inhabitants to pay their tithes and dues to the sequestrators (a direction many complied with, continuing to pay these to Benham, indicating that he had local support). Eventually, after more than three years, the Committee issued a summons to the Sheriff, on 17 September 1647, to obtain possession of Benham's house and to remove him and his wife. Stephen Benham died only a few weeks later, in November, and there is no evidence that he had by then been evicted.

The first specific reference to a Richmond vicarage occurred during Stephen Benham's time, the Manor Court rolls for 1614 referring to 'the house of Stephen Benham, clerk'. This was on what was probably the original site of the manse in Shene, an area of about one acre on what is now Eton Street (there was no path or track between George Street and Paradise Road until the mid-nineteenth century). It seems to have been a modest establishment; the minutes of 16 June 1632 record the Vestry's decision to allow Benham three poles 'to repair his house with'. The first positive reference to this land as the site of the manse occurs in the Manor Court rolls for 1503. However, following Benham's death it ceased to be used as such, the Vestry having decided that the minister should have a better residence and, indeed, they were lobbying for the formal establishment of Richmond as a separate vicarage and parish.

Stephen Benham married, in Richmond on 19 November 1615, Sara Ingram, who was buried on 23 March 1639. On 11 January 1641 he married as his second wife Katherine Riggale. The date of his burial is recorded as 27 November 1647.

Vacancy 1647–51

Following Stephen Benham's death there was a gap of four years, until the next minister was appointed. In the interim the Vestry arranged services on an ad hoc basis.

Jeremiah Benton: 1651–53

Jeremiah Benton, who is thought to have come from Norfolk, was admitted as a sizar (an undergraduate receiving financial help from the college) at Emmanuel College, Cambridge in 1633, graduating in 1637.

Jeremiah Benton was appointed on 1 September 1651. He was appointed by the Vestry, rather than the vicar of Kingston (as was his successor Samuel Hinde), and he seems to have been living in Richmond prior to his appointment as his daughter, Sydney, was baptised there on 18 June 1651. His duties were light – two sermons each Sunday and the sacraments twice a quarter.

Benton's appointment was for one year only, subsequently extended for a second year, but in May 1653 he gave notice to the Vestry that he would be leaving in midsummer. In 1654 he became vicar of Childerditch, Essex; the patron presenting him to that living was Sir Thomas Cheke, a zealous puritan, implying that that too was where Benton's loyalties lay.

It is not known where Benton lived during his short time in Richmond. He was provided with £8 a year for the rent of a house, and negotiations were entered into with a Mrs Child for the lease of her house on the site of what is now Tesco, but there is no evidence that the property was occupied as the vicarage.

Samuel Hinde: 1653–56

Samuel Hinde was appointed minister on 4 July 1653 and, two days later, his son was baptised at Richmond. In making the appointment the Vestry noted Hinde's 'Conformableness to the present Government', emphasising again the sensitivity at this time to the political leanings of ministers. However, there is some evidence to suggest that Hinde's declaration of support for the Parliamentary cause may have lacked complete conviction since, prior to his appointment, he had been chaplain to James Stanley, 7th Earl of Derby, a staunch Royalist who had been beheaded in 1651 for his support of the future Charles II.

Hinde had been admitted sizar at King's College, Cambridge, at Easter 1627 and graduated as BA in 1629.

It is not known when Hinde left Richmond. The last trace of him is a receipt for his stipend as minister for the quarter ending midsummer 1656. He subsequently became vicar of Banstead, Surrey, 1658–60. There is mention of a Rev. Samuel Hinde in *A New History of Dover*, noting that he was appointed to the cure in 1662. He resigned in 1671, the point of contention being that his salary of £100 was 'very indifferently paid'. The reason that the ministry had become vacant at Dover was because the previous incumbent, Rev. John Reading, had been 'ousted during the civil commotions'.

Vacancy: 1656–60

There was a vacancy between Samuel Hinde's departure and the appointment in 1660 of Abiel Borfet. The wall tablet at St Mary Magdalene, listing vicars, indicates that 'William Bradford' was appointed minister in 1658 but this is incorrect, in two respects; his name was Radford and he was almost certainly never appointed minister. William Radford has a short entry in Aubrey's *Brief Lives* (Oxford, 1897 edition, Vol. 2, p.177), in which his friend John Aubrey twice identifies him as a schoolmaster:

> William Radford, my good friend and old acquaintance and fellow collegiate, ended his dayes at Richmond, where he taught schoole, 14 dayes since. I was with him when he first tooke his bed.

> And when I was sick of the small-pox at Trinity College Oxon, he was so kind as to come to me every day and spend severall houres, or I thinke melancholy would have spoyled a scurvey antiquary. He was recounting not many dayes before he dyed your brother Ned's voyage and Mr. Thomas Mariett's to London on foote.

> Mrs Anne Radford, the widowe of Mr. William Radford, schoolmaster of Richmond, is now (1673) 33 yeares old. Was borne the 4th of June at 4h P.M. She haz a solar face (yet the sun in her horoscope could not be *in ascendente*), and thrives well, and has a good sound judgment.

In a report, dated 18 March 1657, submitted to Commissioners appointed by Parliament to inquire into the state of ecclesiastical benefices, it was stated that Richmond was then 'without a settled minister'. It was possibly in response to this that Edward Taylor was appointed as lecturer, 'to preach every Sunday afternoon at Richmond Surrey', to be paid an amount due to a minister, equivalent to £60. Lecturers were occasionally appointed to do service for a minister whilst the latter was away. Lysons, in *The Environs of London, Vol.1* (1792) states that Taylor's appointment was made by Oliver Cromwell.

Radford did conduct some marriage ceremonies in Richmond in 1658 and 1659 and was described on these occasions in the parish registers as 'Minister', and it is from here that confusion over his status almost certainly derives. However, the fact that he continued to live in Richmond after the appointment of Abiel Borfet, and that the Vestry Minutes make no mention of either his appointment or subsequent removal from office, make it unlikely in the extreme that he had been minister at some time between 1657 and 1660.

William Radford came from North Weston in Oxfordshire and attended Winchester College and Trinity College, Oxford, graduating in 1640. That he was living in Richmond by 1657 is evidenced by the appearance of his name, as a father, in the baptismal register for 12 January 1657. On obtaining a licence in 1662 from the Surrey Commissary Court for the teaching of boys he founded the Richmond Grammar School. By 1664 he was living in a house on the site of Nos 8 and 9 The Green (now the office of Richmond Charities Almshouses) and that became the location of his school. He died in October 1673 and was buried in Richmond as 'William Radford, schoolmaster'. His widow was still living in the house in 1679.

The school continued following Radford's death. His son, Vertue Radford had inherited the property and when in 1692 he sold it, the occupant was Christopher Johnson, a schoolmaster (see p.18 regarding his ousting of Rev. Borfet). After Johnson's death in 1710 Rev. Nicholas Brady, the minister at St Mary Magdalene, took over the school (see p.25), continuing as schoolmaster there until 1718. Eventually, in 1764 the then schoolmaster, Rev. Charles Delafosse, established his Richmond Academy in a large house at the corner of Little Green and Duke Street, presumably taking with him his pupils from the Grammar School. Alumni of the Academy include the famous explorer, Richard Burton, whose family lived for a time on Richmond Green.

Abiel Borfet: 1660–96

The next minister, Abiel Borfet, was appointed on 24 June 1660 and he remained in post for 36 years.

He was born in 1633 in Leicester, son of Walter Borfet, and elder brother of Samuel, both of whom were also clergymen. After school at St Paul's he graduated from Christ's College, Cambridge, obtaining his MA in 1656. His first appointment following ordination was as minister of New Brentford, in 1657, a post he retained until his appointment to Richmond. Whilst at Richmond he was also appointed chaplain to Edward Montagu, 1st Earl of Sandwich, and as vicar of Lyminge, Kent, both in 1671. He presumably paid a chaplain to fill his place at Lyminge.

On moving to Richmond Borfet initially lived in a house very near the church, on the site which in the eighteenth century became the Greyhound Inn. His pay, initially £100 a year, was funded by voluntary subscriptions from parishioners, implying that at this time Richmond was regarded as independent of Kingston. Had it been merely a chapel of ease, the provision of a curate would have been the responsibility of the mother church.

As with two previous ministers, Stephen Benham and Samuel Hinde, national politics were to play a part in Abiel Borfet's ministry. His licence was taken away by an Act of the Bishop's Court dated 20 May 1696 and, although there is no formal record of what his offence was, the issue was almost certainly Borfet's suspected leanings towards the deposed Catholic king, James II.

The fact that Borfet had been a strong supporter of the Royalist cause is beyond doubt. In 1660 he had written a poem, a hymn of praise to Charles II, which appeared in an anthology published that year, *The Return of the King: An Anthology of English Poems Commemorating the Restoration of Charles II*. His appointment as chaplain to the Earl of Sandwich provides another clue: Sandwich played a considerable part in the restoration of Charles II. Also, in 1696 he published a defence against swearing an oath of allegiance under the Act for the Better Security of His Majesty's Royal Person 1695; that legislation was enacted in response to a plot to assassinate William III at Brentford. Borfet eventually swore the Solemn Oath, but did so subject to a carefully worded caveat.

The action to have Borfet's licence revoked seems to have been spearheaded by the schoolmaster, Christopher Johnson (see p.16). Johnson was mentioned in 1694 and again in 1696, in documents concerning the case, as a former curate of Richmond; there is no evidence that he was appointed curate, although he had acquired a doctorate in Divinity and on occasion preached at St Mary Magdalene. In 1696, in a preface to some published sermons, he referred to the recently removed Abiel Borfet as follows:

> 'the late Minister of Richmond in Surrey having written, and suffer'd to be dispersed, some Scandalous and Ill Notions, concerning the present Most Happy Government; for which he is deprived of his cure…'

Christopher Johnson is recorded as living in 1692 at the schoolhouse on Richmond Green, and he was still there in 1705. The level of local support behind Johnson's action is unknown, but it is perhaps significant that Borfet continued to live for the rest of his life in Richmond. In 1683 he had moved to a substantial house, in what is now Bridge Street, with a terrace running down to the Thames, and here he was to spend the rest of his days; an unlikely setting had Borfet fallen out with his parishioners.

By way of a postscript to Abiel Borfet's political leanings, it is pertinent to add a few words about his brother Samuel, who also had his problems with the church authorities. On ordination in 1659 he had been appointed rector of High Laver, Essex, but was ejected in 1662, for reasons unknown. Samuel never found another appointment, although he is recorded as having been an itinerant preacher in Maidstone and London. He died in 1698, at Richmond, implying that by then he may have been living with his brother.

Borfet was clearly a man with literary tastes. The Huntington Library has his copy of *The Works of Benjamin Jonson* (1616), a work of more than 1,000 pages, and Borfet wrote detailed comments on almost every page of his copy, adding information, clarifying meanings and recording his responses. At one point, strongly identifying with a speech about friendship, he commented 'True! True to this day', adding his name and the date, 18 May 1696. That date will have been very close to the day he was ousted from being minister at St Mary Magdalene – his successor, Rev. Nicholas Brady, was appointed on 11 June 1696.

He also occasionally wrote verse himself; with what success it is for the reader to decide:

That I, whom Nature never made a Poet,
Nor was adopted once by Art unto it,
Soare above Prose, and force my Novice-Quill
To uncouth Laws against Minervaes will:
It is no marvell, when my Subject's such,
That Art and Nature can't do half so much;
My Matter is my Muse; I find it here
More easie task to write then to forbear.
Fear made the dumb man speak, ...

Abiel Borfet died in Richmond in 1710, aged 77. His wife had predeceased him in 1704. There are baptismal entries for nine children between 1661 and 1673.

An extract from Abiel Borfet's copy of the Works of Ben Jonson

An 18th century minister

Ministers in the 18th century

Nicholas Brady: 1696–1720

Nicholas Brady is the best known of the Richmond vicars. Poet, playwright, chaplain to royalty, schoolmaster, a famous preacher, and someone remembered as a 'true Minister of Christ', he was a man of many parts. Aged 36 when appointed to Richmond in 1696 he had by then already achieved much in his life. He is also, happily, the first minister for whom we have a portrait.

Nicholas Brady was born on 28 October 1659 in Bandon, County Cork. His great-grandfather, Hugh Brady, was the first Protestant bishop of Meath, and his father, Major Nicholas Brady, was a Protestant Irish army officer. He was educated in Cork until, at twelve, he attended Westminster School and subsequently Christ Church, Oxford and Trinity College, Dublin from where he graduated with MA in 1686. He was ordained priest at Cork in 1687 and then became the domestic chaplain to the bishop of Cork, who conferred upon him the livings of Ballymoney, Drinagh and Kilmeen.

Brady then became caught up in the Williamite War in Ireland, the Jacobite response to the overthrow of James II and the Glorious Revolution of 1688. On 24 February 1689 the inhabitants of Bandon, a strongly Protestant town, had evicted the Irish Army garrison, killing some of the redcoats. The town was soon retaken and James II ordered that it be burned. Brady, representing the people of Bandon, managed to get this dreadful command overturned and to have it replaced by a relatively lenient order to pay £1,500. Although he had a strong Protestant background, it is clear that Nicholas Brady had previously been sympathetic to the Jacobite cause – he had preached on the divine right of kings and non-resistance – and as such he was a good interlocutor for these negotiations, listened to with respect by the Jacobite General, Justin McCarthy.

Following the Protestant victory at the Battle of the Boyne in 1690 the people of Bandon chose Brady, with his evident negotiating skills, to represent them before the English parliament in seeking reparations for grievances suffered by them during the Williamite War. He had by now become an ardent supporter

Nicholas Brady

An outgoing man, Nicholas Brady soon established connections within London social circles and determined that his stay should be permanent, relinquishing his Irish preferments. Apart from a fulfilling social life, an added incentive was the prospect of a significantly higher income in England. He became a married man on 29 June 1690 and thoughts of supporting his future family will also have been on his mind. His wife, Laetitia, was the daughter of Richard Synge, archdeacon of Cork, and granddaughter of Edmund Synge, bishop of Cork.

They were to have eight children, although three died in infancy.

Brady was appointed curate of St Katherine Cree church in Aldgate on 16 July 1691 and lecturer of St Michael's, Wood Street. He quickly established a reputation as a fashionable preacher, and the first of many of his sermons to be printed was delivered at St Katherine Cree 26 November 1691, on the occasion of 'the Thanksgiving-day for the preservation of the King and the reduction of Ireland'. Another sermon, on 'Church-musick vindicated', was preached at St Bride's on 22 November 1697, St Cecilia's Day. Including three volumes, published posthumously by his eldest son, over one hundred of Brady's sermons were to appear in print.

Nicholas Brady was also a writer, albeit of mixed success, and it is not too fanciful to think that he will have become well acquainted with his ousted predecessor, Abiel Borfet, with whom he shared literary tastes. For fourteen years after Brady's coming to Richmond Borfet was living close by.

As a writer Brady first tried his hand as a playwright, and his tragedy, *The Rape: or the innocent imposters*, was performed at the Theatre Royal, Drury Lane in 1692. It is fair to say that Brady's links with influential people in the theatrical world, rather than the merits of his work, secured the play's production. It is mostly a rather plodding drama of fifth century Goths and Vandals. Rather surprisingly for a play written by a clergyman it includes a rape scene, albeit enacted offstage. It was not a success but was revived in a toned-down version in 1730 after Brady's death.

Brady's 'Ode on St Cecilia's Day' has proved to be an enduring work, although this is almost wholly attributable to the fact that Henry Purcell set it to music. In 1713 he launched a major project, the publication of a blank-verse translation of Virgil's *Aeneid*, which was published in several volumes between 1714 and 1726. The venture was not widely read and Samuel Johnson was typically acerbic:

> Dr Brady attempted in blank verse a translation of the Eneid, which, when dragged into the world, did not live long enough to cry. I have never seen it, but that such a version there is, or has been, perhaps some old catalogue informed me.

The one work which did receive public acclaim, and for which Brady is mostly remembered today, was a metrical version of the psalms. Written jointly with Nahum Tate the work was dedicated to William III, who showed his satisfaction with it by making an Order, on 3 December 1696, that Brady and Tate's *New Version of the Psalms of David* should be used thereafter 'in all Churches, Chapels and Congregations'. It was widely popular until the mid-nineteenth century. Nahum Tate, Brady's co-author, was poet laureate (1692) and wrote a version of *King Lear* that, throughout the eighteenth century, was performed more widely than Shakespeare's play; Tate's version had a happy end. More famously, he wrote the words to the Christmas carol 'While Shepherds Watched their Flocks by Night'.

Brady came to live in Richmond for a time whilst working on the Psalms, taking a break from clerical duties, and very shortly after Rev. Borfet had been removed from office he was chosen as his successor. He was appointed curate on 11 June 1696, and was to spend the rest of his days in that post. From an unpublished *Life of Dr. Brady*, written by a grandson, we learn that 'he was invited to the living of Richmond by the gentlemen of that place, in consequence of a high esteem they had conceived for him during a retreat which he had made hither'. On moving to Richmond Brady resigned his St Katherine Cree curacy.

It is conceivable that James Butler, second Duke of Ormond, may also have had a part in bringing Brady to Richmond. Brady, who had been appointed chaplain to the Duke of Ormond's Troop of Horse Guards, was acquainted with the Duke, who was a popular national figure and also owned land in Richmond. Indeed, Ormond Road, where the present vicarage stands, was named after him, as was a pub on Richmond Green, *The Duke of Ormond's Head* (now *The Prince's Head*).

Not surprisingly, St Mary Magdalene adopted their minister's version of the Psalms. The Vestry minutes of 22 May 1698 record that:

> Wee The Gentlemen of the Vestry having Seen a new Version of the Psalmes fitted to the Tunes used in churches by Mr. Brady and Mr. Tate together with his Majesties Order of Allowance in Council bareing date at Kensington the 3d of December 1696 doe willingly receive the same and desire that they may be used in our Congregation.

Frustratingly little is recorded of Nicholas Brady's activities as minister during his time in Richmond. The town, and the church's congregation continued to grow during his time there and in 1699 the church had to be enlarged with the addition of a north aisle. William III contributed the not inconsiderable sum of £200, perhaps after persuasion from Brady, his chaplain.

During part of his time in Richmond Brady was a schoolmaster, taking over the running of the Grammar School following Christopher Johnson's death in 1710 (see p.16). One possible motive for this was Brady's need to boost his income, to support his hospitable lifestyle and large family. According to his grandson, Brady's income from all his preferments was £600 (about £120,000 today), but 'his public spirit rendered him careless of his private interest and fortune'. Brady's son, Nicholas, was assistant to his father at the school. A letter from a fourteen-year old pupil, dated 5 September 1711, was published in The *Spectator* singing Brady's praises as a schoolmaster – '... From the gentleman's great tenderness to me and friendship to my father, I am very happy learning from my book with pleasure....It is impossible for any of us to love our own parents better than we do him....'. The letter is certainly touching, although a cynic might conclude that it was principally a plug for the school which Brady had recently taken over.

Some authorities say that Brady was the first schoolmaster of the parish school, founded in 1713 (see p.59) – which was subsequently to become the present Christ's School, on Queen's Road – but there is no evidence to support this. The error presumably arises through a confusion with Brady's involvement with the Grammar School.

Whilst at Richmond Brady also became vicar of Stratford upon Avon, the living being conferred upon him by its patron the Earl of Dorset, and he held that office from 10 November 1702 to 16 October 1705. In 1706 he was presented to the rectory of Holy Trinity, Clapham, a position he retained until his death. Also, he became chaplain to Queen Anne and subsequently to Caroline, Princess of Wales.

On moving to Richmond Brady and his family first lived in a recently built house in Paradise Row. This stood at the corner of the top end of what is now Eton Street, next to Hogarth House. He subsequently moved, on becoming master at the Grammar School in 1710, to live at the school on Richmond Green. He remained there until shortly before his death in 1726 when he moved into a newly built house on the corner of Little Green and Parkshot.

Nicholas Brady died on 20 May 1726, aged 67, and was buried at the parish church.

Richard Coleire: 1726–46

Richard Coleire was born on 14 November 1669 in London, the son of Walter Coleire who, at the time, was the innkeeper of the Magpie off Fetter Lane, and of Lettice, the daughter of Rev. Hugh Humphries, a Staffordshire clergyman. He was educated at both Shrewsbury and Westminster Schools. After obtaining his BA in 1689 and his MA in 1693 he was elected a fellow of All Souls in 1688. He subsequently took holy orders, being ordained deacon in 1692 and priest in 1695. In 1694 he was named as chaplain to Colonel Wyndham's Regiment of Horse (which was on active service in Flanders at this time) and in 1701 he was made Junior Proctor of All Souls.

He was appointed curate for Brightwell, Berkshire in 1699 and, in 1702, he became vicar of Harrietsham, Kent, where he remained until 1716. He also became chaplain to Viscount Falkland (a staunch Jacobite) and to the Dowager Marchioness of Wharton. In 1716 he was presented with the parish of Isleworth which was 'by exchange' for Harrietsham (according to his written statement in a biographical questionnaire). From the notice of his death published in the *London Evening Post* on 28 August 1746, it seems he remained vicar at Isleworth until his death. In 1720 he also became vicar of Kingston, but resigned that post on being given the incumbency of Richmond in 1726. The curious episode of the subsequent lawsuit regarding his appointment to Richmond is recounted at p.4. Rev. Coleire seems to have regarded Richmond as independent from Kingston and his intention was, in his own words, to 'hold it with Isleworth'.

Richard Coleire was married three times, but was survived by only two of his six children, Richard and Lucy, both children of his second marriage to Elizabeth Sampson. By his will, he left the residue of his estate, 'the poor remainder of her handsome fortune', to his widow, Abigail, cutting off his 'undutiful and ungracious son' Richard with a shilling, because of his 'continual wicked and idle life'.

On his move to Harrietsham Coleire became seriously indebted as a result, it seems, of over-ambitious plans to develop the rectory. He therefore had to look elsewhere to boost his income, and became a naval chaplain, serving in at least five different ships, *Medway, Oxford, Expedition, Exeter* and *Bedford*, between 1706 and 1713. Something of a Boy's Own adventure that occurred in 1706, when he was chaplain of the *Medway*, is related in an Admiralty report to the Navy Board dated 3 October 1712.

The *Medway* was at port in Lisbon, and due to sail on the following day, 15 September 1706, when the captain ordered Coleire ashore to bury the coxswain, who had been killed, and to lay before the Consul some depositions relating to the murder. Puzzlingly, the *Medway* then set sail, leaving Coleire and 21 men behind. Stranded, Coleire and his men had then to find their way back to England, and did so by a roundabout route via Madeira, where they obtained passage on a Venetian ship to West Ireland. The purpose of the Admiralty report was to consider Coleire's claim for expenses.

Coleire knew Jonathan Swift, whom he had probably met at Oxford University, and Swift came to stay with him for some weeks at Harrietsham in October 1708. Michael Treadwell in *Swift, Richard Coleire and the Origins of Gulliver's Travels*, makes the wholly credible suggestion that the story that Coleire will have related to him – of an impoverished clergyman, forced to abandon wife and children to go to sea, deserted in a strange land, and obliged to make a roundabout way back to England – will have sown the seed in Swift's mind that grew into the tale of a young physician, Lemuel Gulliver, forced by a failing practice to leave wife and children, and to sail away to his extraordinary adventures.

Coleire's friendship with Swift did not endure, and there is no record of their having met again after 1708. Indeed, there may well have been some falling out between them. As mentioned above, Coleire became chaplain to the Dowager Marchioness of Wharton. Her husband, Thomas Wharton, 1st Marquess of Wharton, who died in 1715, and who had served as Lord Lieutenant of Ireland, was loathed by Swift (not without reason). Swift wrote a diatribe against Wharton, 'The Most Universal Villain I ever knew', so Coleire's acceptance of the chaplaincy will not have endeared him to Swift.

By way of a postscript to the above tale, it is interesting to note that Jonathan Swift has some links with Richmond. In 1689 he became, through a family connection, secretary to Sir William Temple. Temple had houses at Sheen Place (on the site of the old Charterhouse in the Old Deer Park) and Moor Park, Farnham. It was whilst he was at Richmond that Swift first met Esther Johnson, who became a lifelong friend and whom he immortalised as Stella. Esther herself had been born in Richmond on 18 March 1681.

Illustration by Arthur Rackham – *'Gulliver, released from the strings, raises and stretches himself.'*

Many of Richard Coleire's sermons were published, which Michael Treadwell, a professor of English literature, describes as being of 'exemplary mediocrity'. The topics of some of them echo those on which his predecessors at Richmond had focused. On 30 January 1713 he preached at the Temple Church on 'The martyrdom of King Charles I' (see Abiel Borfet). Just over two years later, by which time Coleire evidently had had a change of mind, he preached on the occasion of the day of public thanksgiving for the suppression of the Jacobite rising of 1715. In 1738, on the occasion of 'the erecting of an organ at Isleworth' he preached on 'The Antiquity and Usefulness of instrumental music in the service of God' (see Nicholas Brady). He also addressed issues of immediate concern to the local community, his sermon at Isleworth on 10 February 1722 being 'Occasioned by the Rape and Murder Committed on the Body of Anne Bristow, January 22, on Smallbury Green in the parish.'

On moving to Richmond Richard Coleire first lived in a large mansion, on what is now Little Green, which included among its previous occupants the Marquess of Hertford, Lord Castleton and Lord Scarborough. Perhaps finding this something of a strain on a minister's resources he moved, in 1729–30, to a house on the site of what is now 50 George Street, presently occupied by Kiss the Hippo.

Richard Coleire seems to have been held in high esteem by his parishioners. In 1737 the Vestry awarded him £50 (£10,000 in today's terms) 'as a Mark of their Esteem and Respect, and as an Acknowledgement of his careful and diligent Discharge of his Ministerial Duty for several Years past'.

He died on 21 August 1746, aged 76, after what seems to have been a rich and varied life. Rev. William Comer, Coleire's old foe and his successor at Richmond, eulogised Richard Coleire in his first sermon preached at Richmond on 7 September 1746 (in which he also went somewhat over the top in heaping praise upon the congregation):

> 'My charge is attended with some difficulties more than ordinary… where [also] I am to *succeed* Persons who have been so eminent, who have here acquitted themselves with so much Applause and Approbation, who enjoyed so great a Share of your Favour, and did most certainly deserve it, and who have been so endeared to you for so many years: and some of whose Performances in this Place have been justly admired by all, and can be equalled by few, hardly perhaps by any.'

William Comer: 1746–66

William Comer was born in 1698 in Langford Budfield, Somerset. He matriculated from New Inn Hall, Oxford in 1715 and was ordained deacon on 2 January 1721, and as priest on 21 February 1725. His first appointment was as a preacher, at Hampstead Well Walk chapel. On 22 February 1727 he became vicar at Kingston, a position retained until his death in 1766.

He succeeded Rev. Coleire as minister at Richmond, preaching his first sermon on 7 September 1746. The saga of his apparent attempt to secure the ministry for himself in 1729 is discussed at p.4.

The stories that have come down to us concerning William Comer do not show him in an altogether flattering light. He seems to have been regarded with amusement, but perhaps also affection, by the patron of Kingston, Nicholas Hardinge. Hardinge's son George published a book of his father's poems and other literary output, including two pieces poking gentle fun at Comer. In a note to the publisher, George Hardinge said:

> 'I send you an admirable piece of humour... hit off by the late Mr Hardinge at the cost of Mr Comer, Vicar of Kingston, and at whom he levelled many satirical darts of his Comic Muse. – I never could learn the offence: but, the favourite theme of the satire being avarice, I suppose it was a dispute upon Tithes. He had the general character in our family of penurious habits. I was then a boy; but I have heard some of the neighbours describe him as a man of parts, and an eloquent Preacher. – Politics may have divided them...'.

Comer was a convivial man and clearly not averse to a pint. In one of his satirical pieces, Nicholas Hardinge gives Comer the following lines:

> But I suspect you hoard some liquor
> Fit to refresh a thirsty Vicar

He frequently met up for a drink with James Thomson, the poet, at the Orange Tree in Kew Road. Thomson, author of *Rule Britannia* and *The Seasons* (better known now through Haydn's setting of the German translation – *The Four Seasons*), lived in Richmond and was buried at St Mary Magdalene; his memorial is on the west wall of the south aisle. Something of the spirit of these gatherings is caught by this recollection from a friend of Thomson:

Q - I hear he [Thomson] kept very late hours?

A - No Sir, - very early. - He was always up at sunrise.
– But then he had never been in bed.

James Thomson

During William Comer's time there were many gaps, omissions and mistakes in the births, deaths and marriage registers. These errors are thought to be attributable to the fact that it was Comer's practice to write these up at home in the evening – by when he was too far gone in drink – rather than recording them at the time in church.

The Vestry minutes covering William Comer's years at Richmond reveal some intense local power struggles. The Vestry Clerk, Robert Smith, had died on 10 February 1759 and on the following day Comer named as his successor the deceased Clerk's nephew, Clement Smith. The Vestry were upset with this usurpation of their right, stating that for the previous one hundred and seven years *they* had nominated the Clerk. This heated debate took two years to resolve, a Vestry minute of 9 February 1761 announcing that the Vestry had 'determined to assert and maintain ye Right of the Parishioners in ye choice of their Clerk'. Consequently, the nomination of Clement Smith was revoked, to the effect that 'ye same should be made Null and Void in Law to all intents and purposes ye same as if the said Licence had never been obtained, and the said

Licence has been previously to this meeting cancelled in the Commons and Revoked according to Law'. The Vestry were then free, at last, to make their own nomination, and their unanimous choice was --- Clement Smith. Job done.

Another incident of equal intensity and, at least from this distance in time, pettiness, was the Minute Book war. Since the early seventeenth century there had been two separate bodies responsible for governance of the parish, which covered both church and other local matters. One was the Open Vestry, which consisted of parishioners and which dated back to at least 1596. The other was the Select Vestry, established by the Bishop of Winchester in 1614, which formalised the government of the parish. Part of the reason for the creation of the latter was to put into its hands authority to assess the value of real estate for the purposes of levying money rate; membership consisted principally of local gentry, so this conferred upon them a major say in the rating process. The power of appointing new members of the Select Vestry lay wholly with existing members. The minister and churchwardens were members of both Vestries.

The scope of the authority of each of the two Vestries was never clearly defined although initially the Select Vestry was dominant, including dealing with church matters such as fabric repairs, collection of pew rents and even, during the Commonwealth, the appointment of ministers. But there were numerous clashes between the two Vestries. By the early eighteenth century the Open Vestry was becoming the more important and active of the two; for example, it was that Vestry that established the Richmond workhouse in 1730. And then, in 1749, things came badly off the rails.

The Open Vestry had somehow acquired the Old Minute Book of the Select Vestry, for the period 1614–1715, and at a meeting held on 29 October 1749, chaired by Rev. Comer, the Select Vestry demanded the return of the book. The Open Vestry, also chaired by Rev. Comer, failed to respond. At a meeting on 20 November the Select Committee repeated their demand, and set up a committee to recover the book. The Open Vestry replied that they had arranged for the book to be copied 'in whole or part at the Discretion of Mr Robert Shepheard [a churchwarden]'. The Select Vestry were incensed and, at a meeting on 29 November – at which neither Rev. Comer nor the churchwardens were present – declared the delivery of the minute book to Shepheard to be 'an illegal and unjust act', and served upon 'the Minister and

Churchwardens or' – for good measure – 'any other Persons whatever' notice that they were going to commence legal action for recovery of the book, and for damages. At a meeting, after evensong, on 3 December the Committee for the Recovery of the Old Minute Book announced that they had instructed Counsel. At this point William Comer played his trump card – exercising his authority as chair of the Select Vestry, he refused it the right to meet again and, with that subtle ploy, the saga seems to have come to a conclusion. After the entry regarding that last meeting the minute book is silent, and there is no further mention of the Select Vestry.

At a meeting of the Open Vestry, on 18 December, it was announced that an examination of the Vestry minute books had revealed that the Old Minute Book had in fact been lost, although they had found a copy of the original. The Open Vestry continued with sole authority over parish matters until 1769 when, by an Act of Parliament, a new body of Parish Trustees was created. The Vestry continued with a much reduced role, confined to church matters.

Comer maintained a house in Richmond. Initially, after a brief stay in West Sheen, he lived in a house very close to the church, at the Paradise Road end of Church Walk. Then, in 1749, he moved to the north corner of The Green, where he was to spend the rest of his days. Coincidentally, the first Richmond vicarage was built on the site of Comer's home. Built in 1852, and first occupied by Rev. Harry Dupuis, this remained the vicarage until the move, in 1947, to Ormond Road.

William Comer died on 8 July 1766, aged 68. He was buried at Kingston parish church, and the Latin inscription on his tomb beseeches the reader to recognise both his virtues and his human errors.

George Wakefield: 1767–76

George Wakefield was born in 1719 in Rolleston on Dove, near Burton upon Trent, and after obtaining a BA at Jesus College, Cambridge he was ordained priest on 19 February 1744. His first appointment was as curate, at St Mary's, Nottingham. When the rector of the neighbouring parish of St Nicholas died on 25 April 1749 Wakefield lost no time in seeking the appointment, presenting himself at Lambeth Palace to that end, having obtained the support of the Duke of Newcastle on the way. He was appointed rector of St Nicholas on 26 May 1749 and was to remain there until his move to Richmond in 1766. He also became chaplain to Margaret, Countess Coningsby from 1756 until her death in 1761. The Countess was a great salonnière, her Berkeley Square home a cultural hub for the dissemination of taste, manners and political debate.

Whilst at Nottingham George Wakefield was made a freeman of the town, but he also managed for a time to fall out badly with the corporation. In the general election in 1754 he supported a Whig candidate, John Plumtree, who was standing in opposition to the preferred candidate of both the corporation and the Duke of Newcastle, who was shortly to become prime minister. Plumtree lost but the corporation expressed their outrage at Wakefield's having stood out of line by depriving him for three years of the £20 due to him annually as the incumbent of St Nicholas. Plumtree reciprocated by giving Wakefield the living of Claypole, Lincolnshire (of which he was patron) in 1758, a position he retained until his move to Richmond. The living will have supplemented Wakefield's income but, being a day's ride from Nottingham, he can have visited the church but infrequently; probably a low paid curate was employed to minister to the flock.

George Wakefield was appointed vicar of Kingston on 27 November 1766, following the death of William Comer. Like Comer, he also took on the role of perpetual curate at Richmond (being elected to that position by the Vestry on 16 March 1767) and decided to live in Richmond. He had married Elizabeth Barke in 1749 in Nottingham and they had eight children, including Thomas, who followed his father as minister for Richmond, and Gilbert, who was to become a controversial figure (discussed below).

Information about Wakefield's ministry in Richmond is scarce. But one important development was the installation of the first permanent organ at

St Mary Magdalene, in 1770. Built by Thomas Knight, at a cost of £420 (partly funded by George III), the organ was still in use in 1907, when it was replaced by the present one. The 'Opening' of the new organ on 9th October 1771 was a very grand occasion at St Mary Magdalene, with a performance of Handel's *Messiah*. All four soloists were top rank singers from the world of opera, including the internationally famous (and infamous) castrato, Guisto Ferdinando Tenducci.

Guisto Ferdinando Tenducci

By 1771 Wakefield was living in a house on the site of 34 Sheen Road, which he rented. Following his death the house was bought by one of his daughters, Elizabeth Wakefield, in 1780.

George Wakefield died on 10 February 1776, aged 56, and was buried in the chancel of St Mary Magdalene. His widow was buried with him in February 1800. In the words of his son, Gilbert, he was 'universally beloved for his unaffected manners, unwearied benevolence, and genuine simplicity of character'. There is a monument to George Wakefield on the north wall of

St Mary Magdalene, alongside monuments to two of his sons, Gilbert and Thomas. Gilbert Wakefield was a complex and interesting character and it is appropriate briefly to recount here something of his life.

He was born in 1756, and spent his youth in Richmond. He obtained a scholarship to Jesus College, Cambridge in 1772 where he had a distinguished university career. On graduation in 1778 he followed in the family footsteps by taking holy orders, but quickly became disillusioned with the Christian faith, resigning his curacy within a year of ordination. He spent the next decade employed as a teacher, including a short spell at Richmond, whilst also devoted to a life of scholarship. The first of a prodigious outpouring of publications, which included his translation of the New Testament, appeared in 1788.

He was a man of strong convictions, and his political views became more extreme over the years. One who knew him, Henry Crabb Robinson, described him as a political fanatic – 'He had the pale complexion and mild features of a saint, was a most gentle creature in private life, and a very amiable man, but, when he took part in political or religious controversy, his pen was dipped in gall'. A strong pacifist, and a virulent critic of William Pitt the Younger, he contended that the poor and labouring classes would lose nothing by a French invasion. Eventually he went too far, publishing a Reply to an unremarkable tract that had defended Pitt and the introduction of income tax. In this he accused the civil and ecclesiastical system of corruption, and levelled a string of accusations against the author of the tract, the bishop of Llandaff. He was prosecuted, found guilty, and sentenced to two years in Dorchester gaol.

As an extremist, expressing minority views, Gilbert Wakefield was an easy target for cartoonists such as Gillray. But he was not without supporters. A substantial sum of £5,000 was raised to relieve him and his family of financial worries whilst he was in gaol. And Charles Fox, Pitt's arch-rival, was in regular correspondence with him.

On release from gaol on 29 May 1801, having served his full two-year term, he returned to his home in Hackney, ready to resume his life; a series of lectures on Virgil was planned. Tragically, he then contracted typhus and died on 9 September 1801, aged 45. His body was carried with great ceremony from Hackney through the streets of London to Richmond, where his funeral was conducted by his brother Thomas.

Thomas Wakefield: 1776–1806

Thomas Wakefield was born in Nottingham on 18 December 1751, the second of five sons of George Wakefield and his wife Elizabeth, née Barke. He was educated initially in Kingston and later at Eton, and had contemplated a career in trade until he felt a strong calling to the church. He attended Jesus College, Cambridge in 1774, studying classics and theology, subsequently obtaining a BA.

The Rev.ᵈ Mᵣ Wakefield of Richmond on a Visit
to his Brother Gilbert Wakefield at Cambridge 1770

Thomas Wakefield

Thomas Wakefield was ordained on 6 June 1775 and appointed curate of Kew with Petersham. The appointment was short-lived, as he was appointed to the curacy of Richmond on 1 January 1776, that appointment being made by his father, George, in his capacity of vicar of Kingston. George Wakefield died very shortly afterwards, on 10 February 1776, implying that Thomas's appointment had been speeded by his father's declining health. Surprisingly George Hardinge, the patron of the Vicarage of Kingston-upon-Thames and Sheen otherwise Richmond, litigated, whether or not George Wakefield had the right to make this appointment. The Act of Parliament of 1769 left little room for doubt on the point (see p.5).

The death of his brother Gilbert, in 1801 (see p.36) deeply affected Thomas and for a time he contemplated 'retiring from the world' and renouncing his ministry. Fortunately for St Mary Magdalene he continued as perpetual curate, evidently much loved by his congregation, until his death.

Gilbert Wakefield of Jesus Coll Cambridge 1770

Gilbert Wakefield

The Wakefield family had lived in a house on Sheen Road and opposite them lived Thomas and Margaret Morson, who owned two adjacent houses (now 43 and 45 Sheen Road). Thomas Morson died at about the same time as George Wakefield and, almost two years later, Thomas Wakefield married the widowed Margaret, and moved across the road to No 45, where they continued to live until his death 29 years later. There were no children of the marriage.

Margaret Wakefield

In 1778 the newly wed Thomas and Margaret Wakefield paid a visit to Gilbert, then at Jesus College, Cambridge, and all three of them were sketched by the artist John Downman ARA. Downman, then at the start of his career, appears to have executed portraits of undergraduates who were close friends so they might exchange one with another. Such will have been the arrangement with the Wakefield portraits with the addition of two of Mrs Wakefield, one for each of the brothers. The appearance of Thomas Wakefield is also nicely amplified in an obituary that was published in *The Athenaeum*:

> 'if posterity should wish to be acquainted, though imperfectly, with the mortal form, which was animated by this pure and erect spirit, let them be told that Thomas Wakefield was in height rather

above the middle stature; that the symmetry of his limbs was built upon the plan of strength; that his complexion was dark, as that term stands opposed to fair: that the proportion and the shape of his features were handsome; that the strong intelligence of his countenance was tempered with peculiar mildness; and that when you first saw him you were struck: when you knew him, you were charmed'.

And, as perhaps one might expect, Thomas Wakefield was 'at all times, dressed to meet the eye of his Maker'.

On the evidence of his obituaries in the *Gentleman's Magazine and The Athenaeum*, and of the wording on his Memorial in St Mary Magdalene, Thomas Wakefield was a man whose Christian faith shone through every aspect of his life. A man of whom 'universal benevolence ...was rooted and entwined in every fibre of his heart'. 'His life', we are told,

> 'presented no striking incidents to arrest the common eye' but 'it was like the sun, which vivifies all beneath its beams, or the pure and quiet stream, which, diffusing verdure over the vale, reflects from its even and lucid surface an unbroken image of heaven'.

He declined opportunities of promotion, content with his ministry in Richmond, and in his private life he was retired and studious. Although his own means were relatively modest, he rarely left the house without some coins in his pockets to help needy people he might encounter. He was strongly opposed to slavery and, in a sermon delivered at St Mary Magdalene in 1784, expressed himself in passionate terms:

> Have we navigated and conquered to save, to civilise and instruct: or to oppress, to plunder and to destroy? The Children of the other we daily carry off from the Land of their Nativity, like Sheep for the Slaughter, to return no more: we tear them from every Object of their Affection. Such is the Conduct of us enlightened Englishmen! Reformed Christians!

Thomas Wakefield died on 26 November 1806, aged 54. There is a monument to him on the north wall of St Mary Magdalene.

The Pulpit

The pulpit at St Mary Magdalene has stood in the church for over three hundred years and it is a pleasing thought that most of the vicars discussed in this book have preached from it. In one's mind's eye the long succession of vicars – Nicholas Brady, Richard Coleire, William Comer... Robert Titley, Wilma Roest – can be seen as, in turn, each ascends the staircase, carefully places their notes on the lectern and then begins – 'May the words of my mouth and the thoughts of all our hearts be acceptable to you, O Lord...'. In this happy scenario may the Richmond Vicars be all assembled together.

The nature of sermons has changed significantly over the centuries. The language used, of course, has changed but so too has the length of sermons. Vicars could flow on for well over an hour, and it seems that Rev. Samuel Gandy may sometimes have just been getting into his stride after two (see p.55). Not all adhered to the advice of Martin Luther who, when asked for a brief explanation of how to preach, said:

> First, you must learn to go up to the pulpit. Second, you must know that you should stay there for a time. Third, you must learn to get down again.

The date of the pulpit has not been established with certainty, but there is a reasonable probability it is 1699; the clue lies in the inset medallions on the four side panels. Each medallion contains the family crest and monogram of a member of the local gentry, all of whom were members of a committee appointed by the Vestry in 1699 to oversee the building of a new north aisle (see p.25). The Vestry minutes of 31 May 1699 noted that those works necessitated 'removing the pulpit, reading desk and clerk's pew from its present place to be joined to the south east pillar between the chancel and the nave'. John Cloake suggested that the pulpit may have been damaged when taken down and that the four committee members paid for a new pulpit, the medallions commemorating their benefecence. An alternative, slightly less plausible analysis, is that the pulpit did survive the move, and the medallions are in recognition of the donors' contributions to the north aisle works. The date of the pulpit that was in situ prior to the 1699 works is not known.

The medallion illustrated here shows the crest of Sir Peter Vandeput, 'a dolphin erect, between two wings or', and his monogram, P.V. The three other committee members commemorated are Sir John Buckworth, Sir Charles Hedges and Thomas Ewer.

The pulpit has led a peripatetic existence within the church. Its position prior to 1699 is not recorded but presumably will have been at the north-east end of the nave. After 1699 it remained by the south-east pillar (see the picture of the interior of the church in 1851 at p.52) until when, in 1904, a new chancel was built and it was moved to its present position by the north-east pillar. And there it will remain, usually. Fitted with wheels in 2017, the pulpit is now mobile and free to roam around the church.

The Pulpit today

Rather like the vicarage (see p. 82), the pulpit has been subject to downsizing over time. As can be seen from the 1851 picture referred to above, the pulpit was then raised quite high, with a long flight of steps, and below it were two seats, side by side, for the minister and the parish clerk. Indeed, the Vestry minutes of 31 May 1699 suggest that the pulpit may at that time have been an even more imposing structure, a three-decker, which was common for that period.

Ministers in the 19th century

Thomas Young: 1806–17

Thomas Young, who succeeded Thomas Wakefield in 1806, had local roots, having been born in Turnham Green on 5 October 1769. Prior to his appointment as rector he had already been a curate in Richmond for some years, describing himself, in a letter dated 16 February 1810, as having been 'the unworthy minister [of Richmond parish] for the last fourteen years'. In the title page of a published sermon (discussed below) he adopted the form of 'curate and Sunday lecturer'. And his marriage, to Margaret Louise D'Abbadie, had been at St Mary Magdalene on 29 May 1799.

He attended Emmanuel College, Cambridge, graduating in 1791 and obtaining his MA in 1794. He was ordained deacon on 3 February 1793 and priest on 2 February 1794. His first appointment was on 4 February 1793 as a curate at East Meon in Hampshire.

Whilst at Richmond Young was appointed, on 16 August 1808, as non-resident rector of Cranoe, in Leicestershire, a position he held until he departed from Richmond in 1817, implying there may have been some link between those two appointments. He was also appointed domestic chaplain to Robert Brudenell, 6th Earl of Cardigan, on 16 March 1811.

Information about Thomas Young's time in Richmond is rather scant although a contemporary of his, writing in 1868, remembered him as:

> '… an easy-going man, who managed to get through the whole of the Parish duty, such as was then thought necessary, without injuring his digestion. He was, personally, much liked, but could not have passed muster at the present day. And without irreverence we may say, that one week of the poker-and-tongs work of this time would have been fatal to [him]. It must be recollected, however, that at the time in question, the Curate was not expected to give more than one Sermon on the Sunday, and that the Vestry elected, and the Parish paid, a Clergyman to preach in the afternoon, who was called the Evening Lecturer.'

We can 'hear' his voice, in a sermon that he delivered at St Mary Magdalene on

19 April 1798. Publication of the sermon headed, with rich irony – 'Unanimity and Exertion at the Present Time Recommended' was made at the request of the Vestry, the cost being met by public subscription. At that time Britain was at war with France, and there was the present risk of invasion by the French. Domestically, influenced by the French Revolution, there was radicalisation of ordinary working people and calls for constitutional reform. The mood of the times was famously caught by William Wordsworth - 'Bliss was it in that dawn to be alive'. Against that background Young delivered his strongly patriotic sermon, preaching that Christians owed loyalty to the Crown:

> '...I cannot forbear to pay a just tribute of respect to those Persons who have so nobly stepped forward, at this critical juncture, in defence of every thing that is near and dear to us, as Men, and as Christians, - who have so voluntarily exerted themselves to check the wild Zeal, the false Patriotism, and the restless Spirits of those who wish to disturb the Royal Peace, to interrupt the tranquillity of the State, and to alter the very nature of our glorious Constitution. Let us hope that Unanimity in the common Cause will remove every Apprehension of Alarm from our Minds, and that our Domestic Foes will finally unite with us, to stem the torrent of Destruction with which our Adversaries menace us!'

Coincidentally, the one, short letter from Young that survives, which is referred to above, also relates to the French Revolution. In this letter, to an unknown recipient, he provided the names of 'French Noblesse', émigrées from the French Revolution, on the tombstones in the Vineyard burial ground. He was in fact at that time living very close to the burial ground, in a house just east of the dog-leg in the road where the Vineyard crosses the present Onslow Road.

In 1817 Thomas Young moved on from Richmond, becoming rector of Dodbrooke in Devon and, also in that year, he was appointed rector of Muckton, in Lincolnshire. As with his previous appointment at Cranoe, he will have been a non-resident rector at Muckton, paying a chaplain to oversee his flock in his absence.

Thomas Young's successor, Samuel Whitelock Gandy, was, prior to his appointment, perpetual curate at East Stonehouse in Devon, where he had been since 1799. Almost certainly it was just coincidence that Gandy and Young switched their venues in Devon and Richmond, but possibly it was found to be an arrangement suitable to them both.

Young remained at Dodbrooke until his death in 1828, where he was buried in the chancel of the church. His widow Margaret survived him by 31 years, dying in 1859 in Newton Abbott. There is however a sad footnote. Thomas and Margaret had nine children of which the name of one, John Charles born in July 1820, appeared in a list of names of Poor Orphans of Clergymen, in a Supplement to the Report of 1828 of the Incorporated Society for Clothing, Maintaining, and Educating Poor Orphans of Clergymen of the Established Church. Clearly Thomas Young did not die a wealthy man.

The Georgian South Aisle, viewed from the East, 1807

The Georgian South Aisle,
viewed from the West, 1797

Samuel Whitelock Gandy: 1817–51

Samuel Gandy's family came from Devon, where his father Rev. John Gandy was Prebendary of Exeter, and vicar of St Andrew's, Plymouth from 1769 until his death in 1824, aged 84. Samuel Gandy was baptised at his father's church on 12 January 1776. He went to Eton College and, in 1795, King's College, Cambridge, of which he subsequently became a fellow. He was ordained deacon on 22 September 1799 and priest, very shortly after, on 6 October. His first appointment, made on 9 November 1799, saw him returning to Devon, as perpetual curate at East Stonehouse and St Budeaux, near Plymouth. He was to continue there for the next eighteen years until his appointment to Kingston-upon-Thames. However, it seems that, for at least part of that time, he will have delegated his duties to others since he was an assistant master at Eton from 1800 to 1803.

Samuel Gandy was appointed Vicar of Kingston-upon-Thames on 23 January 1817 following the death of the previous incumbent, Rev. George Savage. Richmond was then still a chapelry of Kingston but, instead of appointing a perpetual curate as successor to Thomas Young, Gandy opted to take on the role himself. However, much of his ministry work in Richmond was put into the hands of a series of young curates who came and went over the years, with mixed success.

Contemporary views give the impression that Samuel Gandy was someone for whom his parishioners felt great warmth, but who was also somewhat unworldly. A local historian, Frederick Merryweather, remembered him as an 'eccentric but genial vicar'. In a letter published in *The Devon and Exeter Gazette* on 12 August 1922 , written by someone who, as a boy, had sung in the choir at Samuel Gandy's funeral seventy years before, he was remembered with great affection. The letter tells us that he left behind 'many who esteemed and beloved him'.

Rev. Edward Hoare who, as a young man, had been one of the Richmond curates appointed by Gandy, held a less positive view:

> 'Mr Gandy was a man altogether incompetent to have the charge …He was a most interesting man, and a deep student of scripture – a man of heavenly mind, one in fact who seemed so occupied with heavenly views that he was unfitted for the practical business of this lower world'

It was a view shared by Rev. Charles Simeon, a leading Cambridge evangelical minister:

> 'All of us are going stumping along on the surface of the earth, but Mr Gandy rises right into Heaven!'

What can be said is that Edward Hoare's barb, that Gandy was a minister 'occupied with heavenly views', was, at least in one sense, wholly correct. From the letter referred to above we learn that Mr Gandy 'was keen on astronomy, and spent many nights on the Church tower with his telescope, noting the movement of the stars'.

The memoirs of Rev. Edward Hoare provide interesting insights to the pastoral state of Richmond at this time. In a letter to his uncle and aunt, dated 19 February 1837, Edward Hoare reported upon the state of the parish as he found it on his arrival in Richmond:

> In all the difficulties and responsibilities of this place I am absolutely alone… I compare myself to a ship finding its way alone across the ocean, and sometimes well-buffeted in the journey… The need of this place is grievous. The little flock is scattered and disheartened; the poor have been totally neglected, the sick unvisited, and the societies are all fallen to decay. The short time that I have been here has not been without its encouragements. Our tender Father has been pleased to favour me with some cases in which my private ministry has been greatly valued, and I hope blessed.

Indeed, shortly before Rev. Hoare's arrival in Richmond there had been a major upset. He was stepping into a void left after two curates had been dismissed in scandalous circumstances and a third had found a position elsewhere.

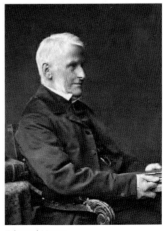

Edward Hoare

Strange Doings in the Church

The scandal involved the alleged misdemeanours of a curate, Rev. Henry Streeton. Streeton, a married man with four children, was rumoured to have attempted to force himself upon Mrs Campbell, the wife of a fellow curate, Rev. Colin Campbell. The matter got into the national press and when *The Morning Chronicle* published an article headed *Strange Doings in the Church* Rev. Streeton sued for libel.

The case came on before a jury in Guildford on 3 August 1836 and was fully reported in the national press. The jury, as directed by the judge, found there to have been no libel, implying that Rev. Streeton had indeed assaulted Mrs Campbell. It is difficult to square some of the evidence with that decision. Throughout the alleged incident, which lasted a quarter of an hour, Mary Longhurst, Mrs Campbell's cook, was in the nursery, immediately above the parlour where the alleged assault took place – 'you can hear, when there, the voice, down below in the parlour: I have heard my master read prayers' – and she heard nothing 'to excite my attention'. The evidence presented to the court seems at times to tiptoe round the possibility that Rev. Streeton and Mrs Campbell may have been having an affair.

The matter also, inevitably, came before the Bishop, Charles Sumner, Bishop of Winchester. He declined to reach any decision on the facts of the case, but declared that neither Streeton nor Campbell should officiate again at Richmond. That might seem a little unfair on Rev. Campbell, but it would make sense if his wife had been on intimate terms with Rev. Streeton.

Rev. Gandy, finding himself now with no curates in Richmond, asked one of his Kingston curates, Rev. John Powell, whether he could step in to take over at St John the Divine. Powell's condition for acceptance was that St John the Divine should be made a separate parish which, indeed, did occur two years later, although Powell was not to become its first vicar. Rev. Powell seems to have been a rather idiosyncratic figure, being described as:

> An able preacher but of rigid economy who often persisted in preaching in the dark because he would only allow the gas to be lit on a certain number of days a year.

After a careful selection exercise Rev. Gandy decided upon Rev. Edward Hoare. Hoare, from the banking dynasty of Hoare & Co, was appointed to Richmond in1837, where he remained for nine years. On leaving Richmond,

A curate preaching on Genesis 1:3 – 'And God said, "Let there be light"' (after Hogarth)

and after some time at Ramsgate, he became vicar of Holy Trinity, Tunbridge Wells, until his death in 1894, a much respected figure at that church. He was certainly from a very different mould than Rev. Streeton, but this did not deter him from causing further upset at Richmond, and discomfort for Rev. Gandy.

All actors are knaves, and actresses harlots

The young, recently ordained, Edward Hoare brought to Richmond his strong evangelical convictions and, as he frankly admitted in later life, he was prone occasionally to overstep the mark:

> In looking back to those days I am thankful to believe that I went to Richmond true to my Master, and I am profoundly thankful for the help given me; but I should make a great mistake if I were to lead anybody to suppose that, in my earnest desire to exalt my Saviour, I never did anything to irritate.

One incident which Edward Hoare may have had in mind, as an occasion that may have 'irritated' others, was a sermon delivered on 25 August 1839, in which he expressed his thoughts on the recently reopened Theatre Royal on Richmond Green. 'All actors are knaves and all actresses harlots', he stormed; 'the Minister of God, like the watchman on the watchtower, has to sound

An 1851 depiction of a baptism in the church, using the 18th century font 53

the alarm when the enemy is at the gate'. Even Shakespeare was off limits – 'it may be that you only attend the more pure pieces, and leave before the performance of the more corrupt parts; but, though by doing so you may, to a certain extent, avoid the corruption to your own soul, you are encouraging the system', a system which presented 'the extreme danger of the weak brother being led into sin…'. Not everybody shared these views. One newspaper responded - 'Who is the REV E HOARE, the Richmond fanatic… [He] is a blind enthusiast or something worse, and should be treated accordingly'. The furious controversy played out over the coming months.

After Richmond, Edward Hoare went on to become a leading figure in the Evangelical party of the Church of England ('one of its kings'). And extreme evangelical views, expressed by earnest young curates, were to surface again at Richmond, in a dramatic way, some years later (see p.67).

Curates aplenty

Further insights into the characters of some of the curates who came and went, with varying degrees of success, during Samuel Gandy's incumbency are nicely described by 'Sexagenarius' in the July 1868 edition of *Richmond Notes*:

> '… they were so many, that without book it is difficult to arrange them chronologically, but we may call to memory the older inhabitants, the Rev. George Quilter, who never smiled; the Rev. Matthew Camidge, gentle and good: the Hon. and Rev. Gerard T. Noel, an accomplished man of narrow views, who lost his way, as Dr. Cumming has done, in the Millenium; the Rev. Sparks Byers retired from the army to join the Church Militant. In his sermons there was often a touching eloquence almost akin to poetry. Then came the Rev. Thomas Snow, a man of homely thoughts and rather course expressions, who once spoke in the pulpit of a "Pot of Ale" as an inducement to act as a sponsor. Mr. Snow was followed by the Rev. Edward Hoare, a strong dogmatist, but unable to see goodness out of his narrow circle of ideas. Then came the Rev. Walter Scott Dumergue, who held the charge until the death of Mr. Gandy in 1851. Of Mr. Dumergue it would be impossible to speak in terms of other than affectionate respect; for although his creed was narrow, there was gentleness

and real spirit of goodness about him that endeared him to all. The kindly nature of his Godfather, Sir Walter Scott, seems to have been imparted to him.'

Rev. Samuel Gandy at Richmond

There is little evidence that Samuel Gandy became much engaged in parish affairs in Richmond, particularly on pastoral matters, although the Minutes of the Vestry show that he sometimes attended meetings. Indeed, there were two significant developments during his time as rector of Richmond, both a consequence of the growing population of the town. Firstly, the decision in 1827 for the need of a new church, resulting in the building of St John the Divine, which was erected in 1831 on land donated by William Selwyn. Secondly, in 1849, the passing of an Act of Parliament finally making Richmond parish wholly separate from Kingston.

Samuel Gandy delivered sermons at St Mary Magdalene from time to time and, indeed, he had the reputation of being a powerful and gifted preacher. In 1859, eight years after his death, a book of his sermons was published, financed by a lengthy list of subscribers, which illustrated the 'endless multiplicity and variety of appropriate and striking images, derived from art and science, from Scripture and philosophy, stored in the inexhaustible magazine of a retentive memory, elaborated by most exquisite taste, and clothed in language that was fascinating and felicitous' that informed his preaching. Many were delivered entirely extempore, and were taken down in short-hand, or written from memory, by churchgoers.

A degree of caution needs to be exercised before accepting that this eulogising of Rev. Gandy the preacher gives the whole story. In a letter dated 24 September 1836 from Rev. Robert Wolfe, Vicar of Cranleigh, suggesting to his son that he might consider applying for the curacy at Richmond, he confided that sometimes Rev. Gandy's sermons could last two hours and that 'some persons when they find it is he who is going to preach have returned out of church.' A copy of the published sermons is held at Richmond Local Studies and, it has to be said, they are not light reading.

It would also be wrong to conclude that the image of a rapt congregation, hanging on the preacher's every word, the only sound the scribbling of the short-hand takers, wholly captures the congregation of St Mary Magdalene from those times. It was sometimes otherwise. For example, the Vestry minutes of 1819 reveal that:

> John Crow Son of Lock Crow of Richmond Shoemaker and Henry Clack Son of Henry Clack of the same place Shoemaker were this day brought before the Vestry on a complaint of letting off Crackers in the Church…

Gandy was also a hymn writer, and he edited *A book of congregational psalmody for the use of the Church of England* (1828). Several of his own hymns were published, including *His be the Victor's Name and What Though Th' Accuser Roar* which, as the following verses illustrate, had a splendid stentorian tone:

> What though th' accuser roar
> Of ills that I have done!
> I know them well, and thousands more:
> Jehovah findeth none.

> Sin, Satan, death appear
> To harass and appall;
> Yet since the gracious Lord is near,
> Backward they go and fall…

Samuel Gandy lived in Kingston. Having let the vicarage there to the church organist, Miss Taylor (who used it as a school), he lodged with a local maltster in a house in Heathen Street, a challenging address for a minister. In his declining years he suffered from 'a painful affliction, which laid him aside, an invalid'. He died on Christmas Day 1851, aged 74. The letter in *The Devon and Exeter Gazette* records that 'he was buried on the eve of New Year with such a display of public mourning, that a brother of his, who came, I think, from Plymouth, declared that greater honour could not have been paid to a Prince'.

Very shortly after his death Heathen Street was renamed, and became – with, surely, posthumous input from Rev. Samuel Whitelock Gandy – Eden Street.

Harry Dupuis: 1852–67

On the death of Rev. Samuel Gandy, Richmond had become a Vicarage wholly separate from Kingston (see p.5) and Harry Dupuis was appointed its first vicar in 1852.

Harry Dupuis was born on 24 March 1808, the youngest of five children of Rev. George Dupuis, rector of Wendlebury in Oxfordshire, and his wife Caroline Elizabeth. He was baptised as Henry Dupuis, on 17 April 1808, but seems to have been known as Harry throughout his life. He was educated at Eton and King's College, Cambridge. On graduating he returned to Eton as an assistant master and remained there until he moved to Richmond in 1852. He was ordained deacon in 1842, and priest in 1843. He married Catherine Rosalie Greene in 1854, and they had five children.

In his student days Harry Dupuis was a keen cricketer, appearing for the Cambridge University XI on three occasions, with a top score of 60. But his final game, on 13/14 May 1830, ended in ignominy – he made a pair.

Richmond was not the first preferment that had been offered to Dupuis, nor the most lucrative, he having bided his time at Eton waiting for a suitably challenging role for fear of becoming, in his words, too 'arm-chairy'. Then Richmond came along. It is possible Dupuis's connection with the Selwyn family influenced his selection as vicar. The Selwyns were a long established and influential Richmond family, and were major benefactors to the church, donating the land on which both St John the Divine and St Matthias were built. George Selwyn had been a master at Eton before becoming Bishop of New Zealand from 1841 to 1868, and then Bishop of Lichfield until his death in 1878. Dupuis worked with Selwyn at Eton and maintained working links with him when the latter went to New Zealand.

Dupuis's arrival in Richmond was apparently awaited by some with apprehension, worried that this new broom might not be to their taste. From an obituary of Dupuis in the *Cambridge Chronicle* we learn that:

> '…his post there was a difficult one; earnest men there had been before him, but no responsible head of the parish –… Fears and unfounded rumours were soon lived down, and before long all honest men were convinced he had but one object – to do to the utmost the work assigned him… For fifteen years he laboured for the

welfare of the rich and poor, though not without discouragement at times…

It must indeed have been a challenging role. With Rev. Gandy being, in effect, an absent vicar, particularly during his last years of ill health, St Mary Magdalene had struggled on with a succession of curates of varying abilities. And, whilst Dupuis came to be loved by many of his parishioners, he clearly was faced by some with strong opinions and loud voices; in the end – as discussed below – the pressures became intense.

Harry Dupuis

During his years at Richmond Harry Dupuis was involved in many aspects of the life of the church and the town. He was the driving force behind the opening of the Richmond Parochial Library and Reading Room, in 1855, 'for the purposes of religious and secular instruction and mutual improvement'; it was a precursor to the Richmond Public Library. He was a mainstay of the Richmond and Kingston Choral Society. And, as chairman of the Vestry he oversaw the decision in 1852 to create a burial ground on land close to Richmond Park, and where he himself was to be buried fifteen years later. Also, on his appointment as a rural dean, Dupuis took a prominent part in diocesan matters.

During Dupuis' time at Richmond there was a burst of building activity; a new home for the Charity School, a new vicarage on Richmond Green, the construction of St Matthias church and major works at St Mary Magdalene.

The Charity School

A free charity school had been established in 1713, situated at the corner of George Street and Brewer's Lane on the site of an old pub, the *Three Pigeons and Lily Pot* (presently occupied by Top Shop). Funded by subscribers that included Queen Anne, it was attached to the parish church. By 1854 – now funded by the National Society for Promoting Religious Education and known as a 'National School' – the school had outgrown its original home and moved to new premises at the top of Eton Street on land that may have formed part of the site of the original manse.

The school was to remain at the Eton Street site until 1960 – by then known as St Mary Magdalene Church of England School – when it moved to Queen's Road. It was renamed Christ's School in 1978.

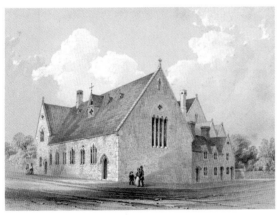

The National School

The new vicarage – Glebe House

One of the conditions in the 1849 Act of Parliament, whereby Richmond finally became a Vicarage distinct from Kingston, was that a suitable residence should be provided for the vicar. Hitherto, ministers in Richmond had had no fixed abode. A plot of land was found, on the north-east side of the Green and, after the Commissioners of H.M. Woods (predecessors of the Crown Estate) had offered this to the parish, construction of 'Glebe House' commenced. This occurred shortly after Dupuis's arrival in Richmond, and a number of his ideas were incorporated into the design of the house. He offered to make a personal subscription to the building fund provided he could appoint the architect himself.

Glebe House was built in 1852 on a grand scale with three-quarters of an acre of grounds and, according to the 1861 census, it then accommodated Harry Dupuis, his wife and three children, together with the butler, a nursemaid, a nurse housemaid and a 'cook domestic'. Glebe House remained the vicarage until 1947 when the move was made to the more compact house (comparatively speaking) in Ormond Road.

Glebe House

St Matthias

St Matthias, proudly towering over Richmond, is the most prominent legacy of Harry Dupuis's ministry at Richmond.

By the middle of the nineteenth century the population of Richmond had doubled in the previous fifty years to 9,255, and to accommodate the growing number of worshippers the building of a new church in the Queen's Road area was considered by the Vestry, which was chaired by Dupuis. Initially this met with some legal objections, on the grounds that the new church should principally benefit the poor of Richmond, whereas the proposed site was in an area occupied mainly by the better-off. That problem was solved when Charles Jasper Selwyn, a Lord Chief Justice of Appeal – gifted a plot of land on the commanding site which, it seems, was then known as 'Mount Ararat', and it was here that the structure, designed by Gilbert Scott, was built. It was consecrated in 1858, although its landmark spire was not completed until 1862. Dupuis was one of the biggest donors towards the building costs.

The large rose window, at the west end of the church, which originally contained clear glass, was filled in with the existing stained glass, in Holy Week 1868, 'in loving memory' of Rev. Harry Dupuis. He had a strong attachment to this newly erected church.

The rose window at
St Matthias church

St Mary Magdalene

With St Matthias built, Dupuis turned his attention to increasing both the capacity of St Mary Magdalene and seating for the poor. At that time there were 900 rented sittings and only 119 free sittings for adults. Dupuis argued that this was 'a great discouragement to the poor' which 'deprived them of their rights'. It is indeed a sobering thought that attendance at church in those days was, for many of the congregation, conditional upon either paying the required pew rents, or of tipping the pew-opener; it was, however, those rents that, to a significant extent, funded the vicar's stipend and church running costs. Harry Dupuis is therefore to be applauded for having increased the capacity of the church, and for having made worship there more available to the less well-off. But those benefits came with big costs – financially, architecturally and, not least, for Harry Dupuis personally.

The works undertaken to increase the church's capacity were on a major scale, involving significant changes both internally and externally. The Georgian, classical character of the church was largely cast to the winds. Some of the long-standing members of the congregation were appalled at the proposals. Some said they would never enter the church again and others offered financial support subject only to the proviso that any funds raised be used to build another chapel-of-ease, leaving the church untouched. Some were in favour of demolishing the church and building a new one. Unbowed, Dupuis pushed on with the plan and, indeed, the scale of the works increased beyond those for which a faculty had been granted. Funds were raised, including a donation from Queen Victoria of £100. Costs escalated, and it then became clear that the project was significantly under-funded. Outraged contractors were left unpaid and Dupuis obtained little assistance from the committees he turned to for help. Relationships with some parishioners became acrimonious. Borrowings had to be arranged to ease the situation, and the church was still fundraising in 1872, five years after Dupuis's death, to clear the debt.

The pressures upon Dupuis were great, and the stress took a heavy toll on him. In the words of one obituarist:

> 'A change came over him – his countenance 'wore the pale cast of thought', his health was steadily declining: still he stood firmly to his post, and attended to the duties of his responsible position

with exemplary punctuality. At length he became seriously ill, and as soon as this became known, much sympathy was expressed. It being known that the involved affairs of the church caused much anxiety of mind to the vicar, several gentlemen conveyed to him (a few days before his death) an assurance that the whole of the remaining debt would be cleared off. When it became known that the symptoms were alarming, the vicarage was besieged by callers, so in order to prevent disturbance, bulletins were posted at the gate with a request 'not to ring the bell'. On Monday morning it ran thus – 'Please do not ring the bell; the vicar has gone to his rest'

The funeral was officiated, at his own request, by the Bishop of Winchester, Charles Sumner, who remembered Harry Dupuis with great affection. He was unable to commence the service 'for several minutes', overcome with emotion.

Although the closing years of Dupuis's ministry were clearly challenging, he was remembered by his parishioners with a very high regard:

'He was a man of purity and integrity of life, of great earnestness of purpose and reality of character, of untiring zeal and hearty co-operation; one who, without great eloquence, spoke from and to the heart; who gained, but never lost, friends, who sympathised with others without a thought of self, and was foremost in originating or furthering any good work.'

In addition to the rose window at St Matthias, there is a monument to Rev. Harry Dupuis at St Mary Magdalene, at the east end of the south wall, and a dedicatory inscription to him on the north sanctuary window. The latter is:

'Dedicated to the glory of God and the memory of Harry Dupuis, B.D., Vicar of this Parish from A.D. 1852–1867, by friends to whom the remembrance of him and his work is still dear after the lapse of 38 years. A.D. MCMV.'

Harry Dupuis was 59 when he died.

Dupuis's widow, Rosalie, remarried, and a word or two should be added here about her future life, and her future husbands. In 1868 she married Charles Jasper Selwyn (the donor of 'Mount Ararat'). In 1870 they had a son, Harry, but Selwyn died shortly before the birth. In 1871 Rosalie married for a third time, to Colonel Francis Hughes-Hallett, another man with a connection with St Mary Magdalene; he was a churchwarden in 1873–75. They had three children, but Rosalie died in 1875, giving birth to the third, Sybil Rosalie (who lived until 1958). Francis Hughes-Hallett was a figure of some interest although, it has to be said, his character was not stereotypically that of a churchwarden.

Francis Hughes-Hallett

Hughes-Hallett became MP for Rochester from 1885 to 1889, and was active in many walks of life. He was a colonel in the Royal Artillery, and saw active service in India. He was an actor of some merit, and used his dramatic skills when travelling in disguise through Morocco, Syria and the Holy Land. He had a pair of performing poodles, Mouton and Don. And he was involved in the staging of Buffalo Bill's Wild West show when it visited London in 1887. He also became actively involved in 1888 in the search for Jack the Ripper, visiting Whitechapel (again, in disguise).

In 1882 Hughes-Hallett remarried, to an American heiress Emilie Page von Schaumberg who, in her prime, had been called the Queen of Washington society. However, he also maintained a relationship with Beatrice Selwyn, Charles Jasper Selwyn's youngest daughter from his first marriage, with whom he was caught in flagrante. Beatrice's eldest brother Charles threatened, inevitably, to horsewhip Hughes-Hallett, should their paths ever again cross in the House of Commons. The scandal received coverage in the national press and one publication, edited by a man whom Hughes-Hallett had beaten in the election for Rochester, proposed that Hughes-Hallett was best suited to be the MP for Sodom and Gomorrah. Hughes-Hallett sued for libel, and lost. He died in 1903.

Charles Procter: 1867–1900

'A devoted, affectionate, and somewhat eccentric Vicar; as holy a man as I know'. Such was the assessment of the Diocesan Bishop, Anthony Thorold, which he confided to his notebook after a visit to the parish on 15 July 1881, adding that Richmond was 'a very important parish admirably and self-denyingly run on rather extreme High Church lines'.

Charles Tickell Procter, who was born on 4 August 1830 at Sandhurst, a son of Lieutenant Colonel Procter of the Royal Military Academy, Sandhurst. He was educated at Eton and King's College, Cambridge, of which he became a fellow. Like the vicars Gandy and Dupuis before him, Procter became a master at Eton (1855–58). He was ordained curate in 1858, and priest in 1859, and prior to his appointment as vicar of Richmond he served as curate at St Edmunds, Salisbury (1858–62), All Saints, Dorchester (1862–67) and Holy Trinity, Windsor (1867). In 1881 he was to be made an honorary canon of Rochester.

Charles Procter

Rev. Procter was instrumental in initiating further building works at St Mary Magdalene. He felt that the church would be enhanced by the replacement of the old Tudor chancel with a new larger chancel. To that end he embarked upon a fundraising exercise and, at the time of his death in 1900, he had received pledges of £3,100. The new chancel was built in 1904, including the addition of two side chapels, at a total cost of £6,872. Designed by G. F. Bodley, a leading church architect of the day, the chancel was erected as a memorial to Charles Procter.

Central to Procter's ministry at Richmond was his concern for the poor of the town. Although both the seating capacity and the free seating at St Mary Magdalene had been recently increased, and St Matthias had been built, Procter felt that the poorest parishioners were inhibited from attending worship, feeling out of place with others in the smartly dressed congregation. To meet that need he initiated the establishment of mission chapels. Some were chapels in public buildings, others more modest arrangements in private homes. The first to open, in 1871, was All Saints Mission Chapel, in Water Lane. Eventually there were thirteen in all, the other principal chapels being St Mary's Mission Room, Red Lion Street (1874), St Augustine's Mission Room, Pensioner's Alley (now Golden Court) (1875) and St Luke's Mission Chapel, The Green (1875). The latter, on the south side of The Green is still standing, although no longer used as a place of worship. However, the mission chapels were not to become a lasting legacy of Procter's ministry, all gradually closing in the early twentieth century. There was no longer a pressing need for separate chapels, class distinctions having changed following the First World War, and with the cost of running them – they were principally funded by private donations – becoming difficult to sustain.

Another way by which the church reached out into the community at this time was through monthly gatherings hosted in people's homes. Initially, during Rev. Dupuis's time, these had been referred to as Cottage Bible Lectures, and the concept was broadened under Charles Procter's direction, becoming the District Visiting Society. The parish was divided into five districts, responsibility for each being allocated between the vicar and his curates. In 1872, for example, there were 34 separate venues across the parish where monthly visits took place. At that time Procter had four curates, shouldering with him the heavy workload of running the parish although, as discussed below, curates were for a time to become a thorn in his flesh.

The Richmond scandal

The fact that clergy played a central role in the life of the town at this time is nicely illustrated by an advertisement that appeared in the *Surrey Comet* on 25 May 1872, placed by Messrs Byrne & Co, photographers in Hill Street, announcing that they were then publishing portraits of the Rev. Procter and his curates. However, photos of the incumbent curates were soon to become collectors' items since, later that year, all were to be instructed by the bishop, in a cause célèbre to become known as 'the Richmond scandal', to depart from Richmond.

The 'scandal' took place against a background of controversy within the Anglican church concerning Ritualism, which sought to reintroduce into the Church of England a range of Catholic liturgical practices. Although, as bishop Thorold observed on his visit some years later, the parish was run on 'rather extreme High Church lines', these were clearly not sufficiently advanced for Charles Procter's curates; in particular, his senior curate, Rev. F. Nutcombe Oxenham.

On Advent Sunday, 1 December 1872, Oxenham preached a sermon at St Matthias. Addressing the congregation at the 11 am service, he admonished them for failing to fast before taking Holy Communion – 'Will you go on seeking a blessing from God in a manner in which He has forbidden you to seek it?'. All, other than those with bodily infirmities, should attend the 7 am service. To do otherwise was pure self-indulgence, and contrary to the authority of Holy Scripture.

This did not go down well with the congregation at St Matthias. Complaints were made to Rev. Procter (who had not been present) and, on the following Sunday he preached at that church, explaining that fasting prior to receiving communion was 'a pious custom, but of no obligation'. The curates were angry that the vicar had not supported Oxenham and furious words were exchanged. The outcome was that Procter said he was no longer able to work with them, and the matter went to the bishop, Samuel 'Soapy Sam' Wilberforce for arbitration. Wilberforce concluded that irreconcilable differences had arisen and that it would be best that the curates should give up their work in the parish.

The story was taken up by the national press, with *The Times* and the *Manchester Guardian* incorrectly reporting that the curates had gone on strike. There had very recently been a general strike of London gas stokers, and *Punch*, in its 4 January 1873 edition, drew parallels between the two:

> '...such a strike is remarkably different from that whereby the Stokers were like to have plunged London into darkness. A general strike of Ritualist Curates would, so far from that, have precisely the opposite effect...'.

Battle raged in the pages of the *Surrey Comet* for a number of weeks with proponents for both the vicar and the curates. Some fell to intemperate ranting - 'He' - the vicar - 'shall go to the grave unhonoured, and, when buried, shall be buried with the burial of a dog', and the congregation at St Matthias was lambasted as being 'content with making Sunday morning a mere dress parade'. The *Church Herald* regarded the whole matter as 'a tumultuous storm in a tea-cup' whilst also observing, of the curates, that 'the clerical gentlemen of that parish are in a pre-Adamite state of chaotic disorder'. But the *Church Herald* spoke with the voice of reason, pointing out that the Church of England was in fact completely silent on the issue of fasting before communion, and suggested that the minor point of principle at issue was possibly used as a stalking-horse for a long suppressed quarrel.

Eventually the matter blew over, the curates having moved on. From this distance in time one's sympathies rather lie with Charles Procter. If he is to be criticised it is perhaps for being too remote from his curates. But Rev. F. Nutcombe Oxenham was clearly not an easy man for any clergy team. In 1875 he published an open letter to William Gladstone on Everlasting Punishment. In 1891 he accepted the English chaplaincy at Rome, and was soon to be found in furious theological controversy with the Bishop of Nicaea. As regards the three younger and impressionable curates who departed with Oxenham, the *Church Herald* perhaps put its finger on it – '... young men fresh from university should not be at once placed in the highly responsible position of spiritual pastor to large and intelligent congregations'.

Whilst the episode can now be viewed as truly 'a storm in a tea-cup', it cannot have been easy to live through for Charles Procter. And it also serves to illustrate the strength of feeling that then existed as to the appropriate form of worship to be adopted by the Richmond churches.

The Vicar's wall

But Procter was no stranger to controversy and no sooner had the Richmond scandal subsided than he was embroiled in another drama, this one of his own making. The saga of 'the Vicar's wall' is touched on by John Cloake, in his history of the Richmond Parish Lands Charity, where he refers to it as 'a truly Trollopian episode'.

By the mid-nineteenth century the lack of space in the Vineyard Passage burial ground was becoming acute, and four acres of land close to Richmond Park (now the Old Burial Ground) had been set aside for the purpose (see p.58). This was part of the Pesthouse Common land which had been given by George III in 1786 for charitable purposes (now Richmond Parish Lands Charity). In 1852 just over an acre of that land had become a burial ground and then in 1870 came the decision to extend it to the remaining three acres. Most of the burial ground was to become consecrated ground apart from one-eighth which was reserved for Nonconformists. It was at this point that Charles Procter – who was clearly a man of means – stepped in with the magnanimous gesture that, if the land were made over to the Ecclesiastical Commissioners, he would at his own expense carry out all the works necessary, an offer that was accepted with alacrity.

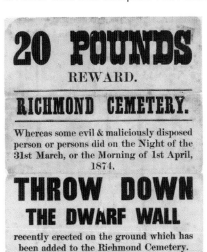

Works commenced in 1874, including building a new access road and a chapel, but only then did the full extent of the works Procter deemed necessary become clear. He had erected a wall, separating the consecrated ground from that reserved for Nonconformists. There was public outcry, but Procter was unmoved. Some people broke in at night and partly destroyed the wall. Procter's response was to offer a reward of £20 (about £2,000 at today's values) for any information leading to conviction of the offenders. Procter's eccentricity, subsequently remarked upon by the bishop, was to the fore. The battle raged on and, as with the Richmond scandal, the bishop again had to step in. He advised Procter to demolish the wall, and so the crisis drew to a close.

It is unfortunate that this unhappy episode seems to have obscured Procter's generosity in funding the works to extend the burial ground particularly if, as seems to have been the case, he also paid the costs of building the small Anglican chapel (now grade II listed) at the Old Burial Ground.

Death of Canon Procter

Charles Procter died of pneumonia on 7 April 1900 aged 69. He had previously been in good health and shortly before his death he had preached twice on the preceding Sunday.

An article in the *Richmond Herald* of 4 November 1916, reporting upon the resignation of Charles Procter's successor, Max Binney, remembered Procter as a man 'who, with all his peculiarities, had a host of admirers and was a devout Churchman'. Evidently much loved by his congregation, he was a man who expected the best of people, whilst himself leading by example. These words from the Bishop of Rochester at a service on 1 November 1904, consecrating the new chancel erected as a memorial to Canon Charles Procter, give a good insight into the character of the man:

> His power with men was… the power of the character which men learn to love along the road of respect mingled with a little fear; the power of the austere bearing, the unworldly fashion; of strictness, vigilant and constant; of principles tenaciously held and unflinchingly avowed; of one unsparing of himself, and much saddened by the sin and shortcomings of the life of his fellows… For remember, while you dedicate this memorial today, that his spirit, if it could speak here, would cry out and say, 'Friends, brothers, children of my flock, if you would give me a memorial, give it me in your lives, in the proof there of whatever through me you learnt of God. Be followers of me, even as I also was, or sought to be, of Christ'.

He was buried at the Old Burial Ground as, subsequently, were all his four sisters.

Ministers of the 20th century

Max Binney: 1900–17

With Max Binney's arrival, at the beginning of the twentieth century, there was a gradual change of approach, away from the Victorian religiosity and values that had previously applied.

Rev. Binney was described as 'truly a broad churchman'. A man 'possessed of moderate views' he 'conducted services with dignity and without any extreme ritual'. In contrast to Canon Procter, who had thought it proper to erect a wall to keep apart the Anglicans and Nonconformists, Rev. Binney invited Nonconformist ministers into the church to attend national thanksgiving services, despite grumbles from the more conservative members of the congregation. A man, therefore, set on breaking walls down.

Max Binney

Maximilian Frederick Breffit Binney was born in December 1859, the son of Thomas Binney who was a parish warden at St Margaret's, Lee in south east London. He attended Uppingham School and King's College, Cambridge from where he graduated with distinction as a Prizeman in 1883. He was ordained deacon in 1883, priest in 1884, and his first appointment was as curate at St Andrew's, Bishop Auckland in County Durham. In 1888 he moved on to become, briefly, vice-principal of the Clergy Training School in Cambridge, moving later that year to become vicar of Sutton, near St Helens in Lancashire, where he remained until his appointment to Richmond. His service of investiture in Richmond was on 19 September 1900.

Very shortly after Rev. Binney's arrival, tragedy struck. His wife, Emily, whom he had married whilst working in Sutton, died on 6 November. They had been living in Bookham whilst renovation works were carried out at the vicarage and on 23 September, after being prematurely confined, she had given birth to their second son George. However, she then caught pneumonia, and passed away.

Rev. Binney came to Richmond with the reputation of 'an energetic and untiring worker', a reputation that was to prove well deserved. However, when the time came for him to move on to another parish, sixteen years later, he explained that 'the time had come for a younger and more energetic man' – a sentiment that was to be echoed by Rev. Barlow, 1946–59, when his time came to leave. This does bring home the point that the pressures placed upon the Richmond vicars are heavy indeed. It is anything but a sinecure.

Rev. Procter had initiated plans for extending the church and had raised £3,100 for the purpose before he died, and Rev. Binney was to see these plans through to fruition in 1904. The works involved a significantly enlarged chancel, in place of the much altered Tudor chancel, and the addition of two chancel aisles and chapels on the south side of the chancel, the All Souls and All Saints chapels. Max Binney funded the building of the All Saints chapel, as a memorial to Emily Binney. The chancel, chancel aisles and side chapels were enriched with fine stained and painted glass, and Rev. Binney funded the window in the All Saints chapel, as a memorial to his father. Other additions overseen by Rev. Binney include the erection of a fine new organ at St Matthias.

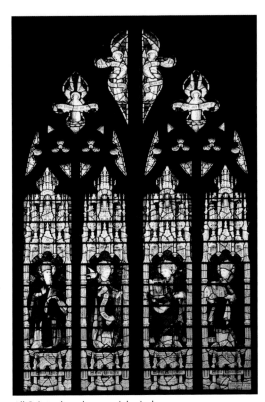
All Saints chapel memorial window

As already mentioned, Rev. Binney had a desire to cultivate relationships with those from other denominations. He was a man said to have 'a breadth of view not all clergymen possess'. His reputation as a mediator travelled far beyond Richmond; May 1915 found him at Donnybrook, acting as 'conductor' for a Quiet Day for the clergy of the United Dioceses of Dublin, Glendalough and Kildare.

Indeed, the window he installed as a memorial to his father may itself be an expression of Max Binney's interdenominational views. It shows four saints and fathers of the church, typical of its four branches, St Basil the Great (the Greek Church), Gregory the Great (the Latin church) St Augustine of Canterbury (the Anglican Church) and St Columba (the Celtic Church).

The windows in the chancel, chancel aisles and side chapels form a coordinated scheme of design and colour which was drawn up by Rev. Binney.

The last three years of Rev. Binney's incumbency saw Britain at war. He ministered to wounded soldiers returning from the front, and organised organ recitals as a diversion from the 'all absorbing pain of the war'. At the outbreak of war in 1914 he wrote in the Parish Magazine 'what a terrible struggle we are all called upon to make. It will test to our utmost our courage and power of endurance and power of making sacrifices. We have got to stand together'. And during the Gallipoli campaign in 1915 he wrote – 'There was never a day when the nations of Europe so needed faith in the resurrection of the dead'.

During his time at Richmond Rev. Binney was Rural Dean, 1901–17, and among other roles he was Commissary to the Falklands Islands, 1905–17, and Argentina, 1910. He was also a member of the Richmond Education Committee, with a particular interest in elementary education.

After sixteen years at Richmond Rev. Binney moved on in 1917 to the quieter parish of Ringwood, on the outskirts of the New Forest, where he was to remain until retirement in 1925. Some were surprised to see him go. Both the *Richmond Herald* and the *Richmond and Twickenham Times* focused upon why he had resigned, and it seems clear that financial pressures, upon both Binney personally and the parish, were an important factor. Possibly he was also experiencing some mental stress. *The Richmond Herald*, noting that the resignation had come upon most people 'with startling suddenness' went to some length to emphasise, rather pointedly, that in going to Ringwood (then, apparently, 'famous for its knitted woollen gloves'), Max Binney was acquiring both a smaller congregation and a larger income. In response to Binney's explanation, that 'the Parish of Richmond ought to have a younger and more energetic man', the *Richmond Herald* tartly responded – 'we cannot help but think he is doing himself an injustice, for he is only just entering upon middle age'.

Notwithstanding the quizzical approach of the local press, all were sorry to see Max Binney go. At a Farewell Presentation Sir George Cave, a parishioner and the then Home Secretary, delivered a tribute, and his statement that Binney had 'set them an example of courage and devotion to duty which endeared him to all the parishioners' met with applause. Binney broke down, and had great difficulty in responding.

Following the loss of his first wife Max Binney had remarried, in 1903, to Miss Lilias Lindsay, with whom he found personal happiness again. She became president of the Richmond branch of the Mother's Union, to which Rev. Binney provided practical and spiritual support. His younger son became Sir George Binney (1900–72) a noted Arctic explorer and, during World War Two, a blockade runner.

Max Binney, by then living in Chelsea, died on 4 March 1936, in his seventy-seventh year.

John Kendall: 1917–28

John Kendall was already known to many of the parishioners before his appointment to Richmond, having often visited the parish as a Lent preacher.

Born on 21 March 1862, Kendall attended Blackheath School and distinguished himself at King's College, Cambridge with a First Class degree in the History Tripos. He was ordained in 1889 and his first appointment was as curate at St Clement's, Notting Hill, 1888–90. In 1890 he became vicar of Little Tew, Oxfordshire and a year later, broadening his horizons, he also became vicar of Great Tew. Then in 1895 he was appointed vicar of Hempstead with Lessingham, Norfolk, a place of which he became very fond, often holidaying there during his time at Richmond, and to where he was to return in his final years. In 1905 he moved on to the incumbency of St Germain's Chapel in Blackheath, where he remained until his move to Richmond.

John Kendall

Whilst at St Germain's Chapel Kendall also returned to the academic world when, in 1915, he became Principal of Queen's College, London, of which he was also Professor of History. This famous independent school for girls, founded in 1848, was the first institution in Great Britain at which girls and young women could study for and gain academic qualifications. The founder of the school, Frederick Denison Maurice, had had to defend himself for teaching women mathematics given 'the dangerous consequences' this would have. Kendall resigned this position shortly after his move to Richmond.

John Kendall combined his Christian faith and his considerable abilities as a historian with the publication of a book, *A Short History of the Church of England* , which he published in 1910. In this short, well-written and well researched work he traced the growth of Christianity in England from its earliest days – which he ascribed to the arrival of Christians in the year 177, fleeing persecution in south-east France – through to the mid-nineteenth century. The book also provides, from an interesting perspective, a panoramic view of English history over this wide timespan.

The *Parish Magazine*, issued monthly during much of the twentieth century, gives helpful insights into the issues that exercised Rev. Kendall and on which he felt it appropriate to address his parishioners. On his coming to Richmond the Great War – '...a righteous war – a war which is being fought for the cause of God ...' – still had almost a year to run. Very often he would discuss national issues such as unemployment, the economy and education, viewed from a Christian perspective. He was, not surprisingly, a strong advocate of education for girls, and the provision of Girls' Welfare Clubs.

Some of Kendall's views were rather of their time. He was against games being played on Sundays, and urged his parishioners to 'constrain others by a gentle love and persuasion'. He also disagreed with a proposed change to the divorce laws in 1919, which would allow those who had been living apart for three years to separate, on the grounds that this would 'alter the atmosphere of every new home'. And he strongly supported the views of Sir Robert Horne, the Minister of Labour, who in 1919 stressed that '...the only safeguard against irretrievable ruin is work, work, work'. It was wrong for a man to seek increased wages since by so doing 'he doesn't bear his share of the burden at all'.

It was a time of economic hardship and another recurring theme was the state of the parish's finances, too often in deficit during these years. Rev.

Kendall's efforts, in this respect, met with marked success, congregational giving increasing by 88% between 1917 and 1926. The following figures are also of interest in showing that at that time the worshippers at St Matthias were those with the deepest pockets.

Congregational Giving

	1917	1926
St Mary Magdalene	£611	£1,064
St Matthias	£1,426	£1,719

The year 1920 saw the election of the first Parochial Church Council for the parish of Richmond. PCCs had recently become part of the structure of the Church of England following legislation passed the previous year – The Church of England Assembly (Powers) Act 1919. The election process was treated with due gravity; the vote counting took a considerable time and, whilst this was going on, the assembled voters were treated to an improvised concert by the Misses Bateman and others.

In November 1927 Rev. Kendall announced that he had been appointed by the Lord Chancellor to be one of the Canons Residentiary in Norwich Cathedral which meant he would have to leave Richmond. He departed the following January, and was to remain at Norwich until his death.

John Kendall died tragically in a road accident on 8 August 1931, aged 70. He was in a car, being driven by his wife, which was in a head-on collision with a bus and he died instantly. Mrs Kendall sustained a broken arm and a broken leg.

George Gray: 1928–46

George Gray was vicar at Richmond during the troubled years of the thirties and forties, the years of the Great Depression and the Second World War. He was remembered by Dr Neil Smith, who had been organist at St Matthias, as 'a quiet, country gentleman type of parson', adding, a little cryptically perhaps, that 'in those days when there were not the same pressures on the clergy to be with-it, he was the right man for the job'.

George Harold Magrath Gray was born in 1881, son of Samuel Gray, chief cashier at the Bank of England. After University College School he went up to King's College, Cambridge (BA 1903, MA 1906), and studied at Berlin University in 1904. He was ordained deacon in 1905, and priest in 1906, and his first appointment was in 1905, as curate of Plumstead, Kent, where he was to remain for nine years. In 1914 he was appointed to St Barnabas, Southfields and then, in 1916, he became vicar of St Bartholomew's, Battersea.

In 1922 George Gray went to South Africa, becoming rector of St Peter's, Vryheid, a 'small but dignified' church which had been built in 1914. In 1924 he moved on to become Principal of Zulu Theological College, a training college that had been set up by the second bishop of Zululand in 1880. He remained there until his appointment as vicar of Richmond in 1928, although, as Commissary for Zululand and Swaziland, he maintained links with South Africa.

On his arrival in Richmond Rev. Gray had a nasty shock. It was the case in those days that the incumbent was liable to meet dilapidation costs at the vicarage, and the Diocesan Dilapidations Board announced that he owed them £246 (broadly equivalent to a year's pay). He appealed to his parishioners for help and some contributions were made, although it seems he had to pay the greater part himself.

In his eighteen years at Richmond Rev. Gray had to address both national and local issues. With the onset of the Great Depression in 1931 he urged that 'the people must support the state and not the state the people'. As regards unemployment people should 'think and pray and act as your means allow'. At Passiontide, in 1930, when there was an outdoor procession at 7.00 am, he said that 'we have to bear our own witness to the fact that the world needs more than education and civilisation, it needs redemption'.

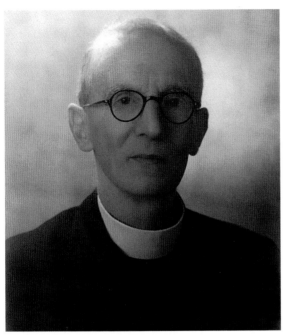
George Gray

In 1945, as the Second World War finally drew to a close, Rev. Gray set up a Welcome Committee to arrange social events for returning servicemen. 'We know that those on service are looking forward to taking part in them' he said, and that to 'start getting our peace-time way of life going again is not to forget them but to help them in securing for them and for us all the things for which they are fighting'.

At the local level, activities on the sabbath again came to the fore. In 1932 there was a proposal for cinemas to be open on Sundays, and Rev. Gray took a strong, albeit unsuccessful, stand against this. In his view the cinemas were not interested in the public, their only goal being to make more money at the cost of 'the destruction of what is of inestimable value in the national life'.

As was to be the case with his successor, Rev. Barlow, George Gray's time at Richmond was to be one of ongoing financial hardship. Year after year the Treasurer's Report announced that deficits had arisen, and there were regular appeals for funds. In 1928 Rev. Gray introduced a system of Freewill Offering encouraging, for the first time, regular weekly giving from members of the congregation.

There were also intense pressures on clergy time, even with four or sometimes five curates. As Rev. Gray explained – 'St Matthias is not like an ordinary daughter church, we are really two parishes in one and two priests are needed for each church'. In addition, clergy had to attend at other institutions, such as the Royal Star & Garter Home and the Grove Garden Hospital (located in the eighteenth century Workhouse).

Notwithstanding these pressures Rev. Gray was anxious to reach out to the citizens of Richmond, to visitors and to children. Sunday evening services were held, weather permitting, by the river and at the Band Stand in Terrace Gardens. And arrangements were made so that the two churches should be open every day, from early service until dusk. In 1933 a system of At Homes was set up, whereby people were invited to social events at parishioners' homes. And in 1934 the Richmond Youth Campaign was launched.

By 1931 the churchyard had fallen into a sorry state and Rev. Gray proposed that improvements needed to be made. The intention was that it should become 'a veritable beauty spot and provide rest to the eyes that would form the complement to the rest of mind obtainable within the old Church'. A major tidy up was duly carried out and among the rubbish removed was 'part of a bedstead, a motor cycle driving belt, a large petrol funnel, a leg of mutton (whole), several loaves of bread, half a bicycle, and a cart load of sardine and other tins.'

Another important improvement carried out by Rev. Gray, the removal of a gallery, was to have a transformative effect upon the interior of the church. The gallery, erected in 1866 at the west end of the church, had created a dark, cramped space, and its removal brought back a pleasing sense of spaciousness and dignity which had been lost. This also revealed again what had been hidden from view, the fine Tudor arch, the only remaining portion of the fifteenth century church to be seen inside, and several old monuments. Rev. Gray carried out all these improvements as a memorial to his wife, Beatrice, who had died in 1934; there is a plaque commemorating the gift of George Gray, 'in grateful memory of his beloved wife', on the South wall of the West porch.

Gray was made Rural Dean of Richmond and Barnes in 1937 and Honorary Canon of Southwark Cathedral in 1940, holding both positions until 1946.

On leaving Richmond, Rev. Gray became Canon Emeritus and moved to Ely, where he preached part time. He moved to Chelmsford in 1952 and then in 1959 to Chichester where he stayed until 1965. During his last years he lived at Cranbrook in Kent. He died on 16 November 1970, aged 89.

Montague Barlow: 1946–59

Montague Barlow was born in Cambridge in 1898, son of Rev. Henry Barlow and grandson of Rev. William Barlow, dean of Peterborough. He was a nephew of Sir Anderson Montague-Barlow, who chaired the Barlow Commission (1942) that reported on urban concentration of population and industry. His maternal grandfather was a professor at King's College, Cambridge.

Montague Barlow

In his schooldays Montague Barlow was a chorister in the King's College choir, but he decided upon Oxford for his degree, graduating from Brasenose College, BA in 1921 and MA 1925. After training at Westcott House, Cambridge he was ordained deacon in 1924 and priest in 1925. He was to spend the first twenty three years of his priesthood in the north of England, eleven in Cumbria and the remainder in Northumberland. On ordination he was appointed curate of Stanwix, 1924–28, followed by Penrith, 1928–31, after which he became vicar of Millom with Kirksanton, 1931–35. In 1935 he was appointed vicar of St Andrew's, Corbridge, where he remained until his move to Richmond in 1947. St Andrew's, Corbridge, in Hadrian's Wall territory, is an ancient church that had originally been built in about 674. Whilst at St Andrew's Rev. Barlow was a representative for Newcastle Diocese in Convocation and the National Church Assembly.

On Rev. Barlow's arrival in 1947 he, together with his wife and their four daughters, ranging in age from ten years to fifteen months, moved into the new vicarage, Ormond Lodge. The previous vicarage, Glebe House, built in 1852 (see p.59), was a mansion with its own ballroom and two tennis courts and no longer an entirely suitable home for a vicar. It was converted into accommodation for parish clergy and remained so until sold, by the Diocese, in 1967. Half the proceeds were used to purchase Ormond Lodge which until then had been owned by the Sandover Trust, a charitable trust created by William Sandover in 1902, and the other half was used to renovate Ormond Lodge. Prior to the Barlow family moving to Ormond Lodge it had been used as a Working Men's Club and for other social purposes.

Biographical detail on Rev. Barlow, telling us something about his character, is frustratingly elusive. In his Vicar's Letter in the monthly *Parish Magazine* he rarely strayed from discussing the forthcoming seasons and feast days of the liturgical year, whereas other vicars have tended to be more informal. He had high expectations of his parishioners:

> 'I believe that the primary duty and privilege of the Christian layman is to come to Holy Communion every Sunday and then at the end of the day to be present at Evening Prayer.'

It is clear that Rev. Barlow had a very heavy workload. Writing in 1949 he said:

> 'It will be two years on February 1 since my institution and induction here as Vicar and I am just beginning to find my feet even if the pressure of work is so great that I find it sometimes very difficult to keep on them.'

One major event at St. Mary Magdalene during these years, when the church was full to overflowing, was the sad occasion of the memorial service, in

February 1952, for the recently departed George VI.

Looking back on his twelve years at Richmond, in his farewell letter, Rev. Barlow specifically mentioned the continuous restorations and alterations at the two churches, and at Ormond Lodge and Glebe House, that had so frequently concerned him. It was also a challenging time financially, and badly needed works often had to be delayed. In 1953 it became necessary to obtain a bank loan, and also a loan from the Diocese, to deal with beetle in the roof at St Mary Magdalene. In the January 1953 parish magazine Rev. Barlow made the position very clear – '...we are literally living from hand to mouth...'. In January 1955 he was urging that 'we have got to think of every house being visited in order to gain support for the Restoration Fund'.

The closing words of his final Vicar's Letter were that 'there is no question of the fact that Richmond is a very heavy task... but it does need someone a little younger'. He was then aged 61.

On leaving Richmond Rev. Barlow became rector of St Mary the Virgin in Buckland (which is between Dorking and Reigate) where he was to remain until retirement in 1967. He spent most of his retirement years in Suffolk, with permission to officiate within the Diocese of St Edmundsbury and Ipswich, 1967–90. In his final years he moved to Kent, with permission to officiate in Canterbury Diocese. He died in 1990 aged 92.

Derek Landreth: 1959–70

'If you want to learn how to run a parish' stated Mervyn Stockwood, Bishop of Southwark, 'look at Derek Landreth'. He was remembered as a man who organised with a military precision.

Derek Landreth was born on 17 June 1920 and was brought up as a Methodist. His father, Rev. Norman Landreth, was a Methodist minister (he was to become vicar of Carshalton Methodist Church in 1936) and he sent his son to Kingswood, the Methodist school in Bath. However, by the 1930s Kingswood was accepting pupils from other denominations, and Derek Landreth found himself strongly drawn towards Anglicanism.

Derek Landreth

On leaving school Landreth was accepted for ordination training but the Second World War intervened and he joined the army. He served in the Royal Corps of Signals and as a Captain in the Royal Artillery, on active service in India and Burma until 1946. Sadly, his brother was killed on active service during the war. Rev. Landreth was to retain strong, and fond, links with the military in later years, becoming chaplain to the Territorial Army, 1951–75, and receiving the Territorial Decoration in 1963. He was also remembered in Richmond as 'a military man' both for his precise organising skills, and for the fact that he was never known to miss an opportunity to put on his uniform.

On demobilisation he went up to King's College, Cambridge, where he read history, BA in 1947 and MA in 1952, and then to Bishop's College, Cheshunt in training for ordination. His first appointment on ordination, in 1948, was as curate at St Hilda's, Crofton Park, followed by St George's, Camberwell, then a working-class community recovering from the war. In 1953 he moved on to become vicar of St Mark's, Battersea Rise and, whilst there, he was also deputy chaplain to Wandsworth prison.

Rev. Landreth was appointed to Richmond in 1959. He was regarded as a powerful and straightforward preacher, whose sermons were 'both profound and rooted in everyday experience'. Although some remembered him for his sense of humour, he clearly also had an austere side to him. A parishioner still vividly remembered Rev. Landreth, fifty years later, as an 'inspiring vicar whose glance at an errant fourteen-year old server could bring one out in a cold sweat'.

Rev. Landreth was keen to establish ecumenical contacts between the churches and clergy of the town and, to that end, he set up the Richmond Ecumenical Council. This was to lead him in an unexpected direction. The Ecumenical Council came to the view that the town was in danger of becoming something of a ghetto for the elderly, and that some way must be found for providing affordable housing for the young. One of the members, the Barn Church, Kew, raised the issue of the land in Queen's Road, beside Richmond Park, which had been given to the Richmond Parish Lands Charity by George III in 1786. At that time, in 1962, the Council were acting as trustee of the charity, and they had been rather secretive as to their intentions with regard to the land. It was rumoured that they were planning to sell it off for development to the highest bidder, whereas the Ecumenical Council took the view that it should be redeveloped for the good of the community.

As chair of the Ecumenical Council, Rev. Landreth set up a meeting with councillors. They listened to him with due courtesy, and then replied 'Let the Vicar of Richmond dirty his hands and come down into the muck of politics instead of standing on the sidelines… they are back-seat drivers'. Rev. Landreth had an answer to this – he would sit behind the wheel. Local elections were due in May 1963 and Derek Landreth stood, and was elected, as an independent member. The Conservatives lost their majority, and the balance of power now lay with Derek Landreth, together with some other independent members.

Although the issue of the use of the Queen's Road land proved tortuous and was to take some years to resolve, Rev. Landreth's appointment as a councillor was a key turning point. Eventually, in 1978, after a court case (won on appeal in the Court of Appeal), the creation of a new trust to widen the scope of the 1786 charity, and struggles with planning regulations, the wishes of the Ecumenical Council, and of the many able and committed individuals who also entered the fray, were fulfilled. Works then commenced on Phase 1 of the Queen's Road Estate development, which was to include social housing and land used for charitable purposes at a nominal rent.

In 1970 the Bishop asked Rev. Landreth to take on Sanderstead, a parish then in need of a revival in its fortunes. He continued there until 1977, after having set up a Team Ministry for the three churches in the parish.

During Mervyn Stockwood's time Southwark Diocese was a close-knit family and Rev. Derek Landreth became one of the Diocesan patriarchs. In 1977 he became a full-time executive at the Diocese, taking on the challenging role of vice-chairman of the Diocesan Pastoral Committee. In 1980 he was elected to represent the clergy of the Diocese at General Synod and also, that year, he was appointed Chaplain to the Queen. Sadly, he had been in post for only four years when his wife, Joan, had a severe stroke. Needing more time to care for her, he moved to a lighter post, becoming vicar of Icklesham in 1982, and rural dean for Rye.

After Joan's death Derek Landreth married Deaconess Isabel White, whom he had met at Sanderstead. They had eighteen months working together at Icklesham until retirement in 1988. They then moved to Slindon, near Arundel, and enjoyed many happy years together. Derek became a member of the local cricket club and the horticultural society. Between studying military history, and trips to the Arctic and the Indonesian Archipelago, Derek Landreth also took up riding again. And then after a very full life, aged 80, Canon Landreth looked heavenward – his first ascent in a hot-air balloon.

Derek Landreth died, on 25 January 2003, aged 82.

John Oates: 1970–84

John Oates was born in Flockton, Yorks on 14 May 1930, son of John and Ethel Oates. He went to Queen Elizabeth School, Wakefield and was called up for National Service (RAF) at 18. He had plans for going to university, but his mother's sudden death lead to an abrupt change of course. Ethel was a Catholic and there had previously been tensions with both Ethel's family and the Roman Catholic priesthood. The news, delivered on the day of her funeral, that a Roman Catholic priest was willing to say prayers over her grave provided she was not taken into an Anglican church first, lead to great bitterness and recriminations. Looking for a complete break, John Oates decided to travel.

John Oates

Arriving in Australia a few weeks after leaving the RAF he was to come across the theological college of the Society of the Sacred Mission and, impressed by its unique way of training young men for the priesthood, applied and took the option of attending the Society's theological college in England, at Kelham. He was ordained deacon in 1957 and priest in 1958.

His curacy was at St Mary of Eton, Hackney Wick, 1957–60. Here, concerned at the low level of activity at the Youth Club, with only twelve members, he organised a complete revamp of the club in 1959 and managed to persuade Cliff Richard to open it. There were 450 people there on the opening night, and club membership subsequently increased significantly. Indeed, 'The 59 Club' is still running today, albeit having now been transformed into a motorbike club.

On leaving Hackney Wick, John Oates was to spend the following decade at Church House and it was during this time, in 1962, that he married Sylvia. His first appointment was as Development Officer of the Church of England Youth Council, 1960–64, helping with the development of Parish Youth Centres, building on his experience with Hackney Wick. He then became Secretary of the Committee on Migration and International Affairs, a position he held until his induction as vicar of Richmond in December 1970.

Some had reservations, on learning of John Oates' appointment in 1970, concerned whether after ten years at Church House he would be the right man for the job; he was soon to dispel their worries. He brought to Richmond a breadth of vision for the parish, together with an ability to drive things forward. He was to have a transformative effect at the three churches, and also deepened the church's involvement in social issues in the town.

Richmond Parish

When built, in 1831, St John the Divine had been a chapel of ease to the parish church, St. Mary Magdalene, but was shortly to become the parish church of a new and separate parish. One important development during John Oates' tenure was that, in 1976, St John the Divine was reunited with the parish of Richmond, which by then included St Matthias. The combined parish now contained three large churches and John Oates needed to address how best to utilise them.

St Matthias

Various proposals had been floated in past years regarding St Matthias. One idea had been to build a new church hall on the land at the east end of the church. In 1971 John Oates set up a commission to explore how the pastoral and community needs of those living on the Hill could be better met by the church. Following a feasibility study Richmond Parish Lands Charity agreed to contribute ninety percent of the costs, and works commenced in 1977. The completed scheme included the removal of all the pews from the nave and aisles, a new floor, self-contained rooms and spaces at two levels around three sides of the west end of the building, including a kitchen and lavatories.

St John the Divine

For some years St John the Divine had been experiencing a shrinking congregation and one proposal that had been actively pursued, shortly prior to John Oates' arrival, was to convert the lower part of the church into offices with a church above; indeed, a planning application had been submitted with the intention of putting this into effect.

John Oates was convinced that St John the Divine had a positive future, and the conversion proposal was dropped. Rather than decommissioning part of the church, it was to be expanded and refurbished. Fortuitously, land at the corner of Church Road and Kew Road came up for development at that time and, working with Bishop Mervyn Stockwood, John Oates negotiated with the developer for a sale of a strip of land owned by the church. The proceeds were to pay for extensive works, including a new church hall, significant refurbishment work and, attached to but separate from the church, St John's Lodge, flats for social housing (presently occupied by SPEAR, the charity for homeless people).

The revived St John the Divine, which maintains a distinctly Catholic tradition in its liturgy and music, was to experience a period of new growth.

The public face of the Church

John Oates was keen to promote the public face of the church and to that end, he established links with businesses, cultural organisations and charities. The vicarage in Ormond Road which, hitherto, had been rather off-limits to most people, adopted a much more open-house approach. The main rooms on the first floor were adapted for social events, meetings and so on, whilst the Oates family found the basement much better suited to everyday family life. As chaplain to the Richmond Theatre, John Oates would welcome the actors after the Wednesday matinee performance for an afternoon cup of tea. He was also to become chaplain to three Richmond mayors.

One event that has stayed in many people's memories was John Oates' promotion of MIND Week, a national campaign. Mounted upon an elephant, which had been arranged by Sylvia with Billy Smart's Circus – Billy Smart was a friend from The 59 Club days – he paraded along George Street, generating huge media coverage. The successful outcome of the campaign was the establishment of two 'Half Way Houses' in Kew Road.

Another of Sylvia's brainwaves was the creation of the Richmond May Fair. Organised within five months of John Oates' induction, the Medieval May Fayre was held on 1 May 1971. With stallholders in appropriate costumes, blissful weather and 15,000 visitors, it was a huge success. For the first few years the May Fair was located around St Mary Magdalene church but, whilst the church remained its heartbeat, it was soon to extend out onto The Green and in one year, to commemorate the bicentenary of Richmond Bridge, to the riverside.

John Oates also played a very active role in local civic and social issues. In the colourful language of the *Richmond Herald* of 27 December 1973:

> 'Whenever anything stirs in his parish ...... John Oates seems to glide in on the scene with his wide cloak flapping at his heels and make his presence felt in no uncertain terms'.

The Richmond Riverside site had become a rather run-down area, and the derelict Palm Court Hotel was partly occupied as a home for battered wives. John Oates heightened discussion around the plight of the women, speaking publicly on the issue and taking the bishop of Southwark around the site.

John Oates regarded training curates as an important part of his mission and Richmond parish was consequently designated a Training Parish. Lyle Dennen and Paul Wright both went on to become archdeacons (of Hackney and of Bromley and Bexley respectively) and Christopher Lowson became Bishop of Lincoln.

Daily morning services were introduced, enabling people to attend worship before going to work. On a more public scale, there were live TV broadcasts of services at both St John the Divine and St Mary Magdalene, and the latter was also privileged to have a visit by the Choir of King's College, Cambridge, conducted by David Willcocks.

After Richmond

In 1984, after fourteen years at Richmond, John Oates moved on to the important post of rector of St Bride's, Fleet Street – 'For anything less than St Bride's, I would never have left!'. He was to arrive at a difficult time. Known as the cathedral of Fleet Street, St Bride's had for many years been closely associated with journalists and newspapers but, by 1989, following Rupert Murdoch's defeat of the striking newspaper workers, all of the national papers had moved elsewhere. During the Wapping dispute John Oates found himself very much at the centre of things, with both the print chapel and the proprietors looking to him for support.

Margaret Thatcher, attending a memorial service at St Bride's, with Canon Oates

Although the newspapers had departed, John Oates managed to maintain St Bride's pre-eminent position in the journalistic and media world. Memorial services were held for journalists and broadcasters killed whilst working overseas, such as the stoning and hacking to death of four young newsmen in the Somalia civil war – a service attended by the world's media. The thanksgiving service for the release of John McCarthy was attended by the prime minister, John Major and the leader of the opposition, Neil Kinnock, and prime ministers Thatcher and Blair also came to some memorial services of national significance.

In 1997 John Oates became both Area Dean for the City and Prebendary at St Paul's Cathedral, positions he was to retain until retirement on 2000, when he became Prebendary Emeritus. He was made a Freeman of the City of London in 1985, and made Canon of St Boniface Cathedral, Bunbury in 1968.

On John Oates' retirement Viscount Rothermere hosted a dinner at Claridge's for 200 leading members of the media at which Charles Moore, editor of *The Daily Telegraph*, gave the address and presented him with a Matt cartoon with two newsmen outside El Vino, the popular Fleet Street watering hole, saying - 'Let's go to St Bride's, the service is better'.

Bruce Carpenter: 1984–91

Bruce Carpenter was born in 1932 in East Cowes, Isle of Wight, the sixth of seven children, and lived there until he was nine, when his home was bombed. The family moved to Ryde, where Bruce joined the church choir and eventually became head chorister. After grammar school in Sandown he took a BA degree in French and Spanish through London University, graduating in 1954. This included one year at Montpellier University and one year at the Sorbonne University in Paris

Then, aged 21, he joined the Navy, for National Service, and trained as a Russian interpreter, spending a year in Cornwall and a year in Kiel, Germany. During that time, whilst reading the bible alone on watch, thoughts of ordination formed in his mind, but he decided to take it slowly. Coming out of the Navy he took a teaching post in a secondary school on the Isle of Wight, and two years later qualified as a teacher.

In due course, Bruce trained for the ministry and returned to university, this time in Durham, to study Theology and Ministry Training at St Chad's College, and he was ordained deacon in 1959, and priest in 1960. He served two curacies (which was normal at that time), each of four years, one at St Mark's, Portsmouth and the next at St Peter and St Paul in Fareham. It was during this second curacy that he met his wife, Angela (a young teacher) and they were married by the Bishop of Portsmouth in 1967, just before he took up his first post as vicar of St John the Baptist, Locks Heath, between Fareham and Southampton.

Bruce Carpenter was at Locks Heath for seven years, and his three children were all born during that time. He also became a member of General Synod and was made Rural Dean of Fareham and Gosport. Next he was asked by the Bishop to become Rector of the first Team Ministry in the Portsmouth diocese, which was based on Holy Trinity Church, Fareham. He spent ten 'immensely happy' years there, establishing a Team Ministry during that time.

In 1984, his appointment at Fareham coming to an end, Bruce Carpenter applied to fill the vacancy at Richmond. The patron, King's College, Cambridge, was hoping Richmond parish would become a Team Ministry, changing it from the traditional set-up of one vicar with curates for the three churches. There were sixty five applicants and Bruce Carpenter, with his working knowledge of Team Ministries, was the right man for the job.

Bruce Carpenter

Whilst at Richmond Bruce Carpenter had a very special time when he was asked by the Archbishop to take part in an exchange with a Russian Orthodox priest. And this led to an amusing incident at the Christmas Day service at St Mary Magdalene. A small party of Russians, none of them English speakers, had come to stay at the Vicarage and they attended the service. Also in the congregation was a little boy who was keen to play with his new fire-engine and at several points during the service confusion reigned as the Russian party gravely rose to their feet assuming that the fire-engine bell signified important moments of worship.

A more solemn incident at the church – albeit one with a happy ending – was the occasion on which Bruce Carpenter was ceremoniously carried out from the vestry, through the congregation of the 8am Communion Service, having had a suspected heart attack when robing. In fact, he had been taken ill with gallstones and was very soon back in harness.

Much was done to work towards the creation of a Team Ministry. As Bruce Carpenter explained at the time, the most important benefit of a Team Ministry is to provide long-term stability for the parish, and with a Team there is less clerical domination, which helps to draw out the role of the lay people – 'The laity are not there to help the clergy run the church. The clergy are there to help the laity be the church'. Although Richmond was not formally to become a Team Ministry until 1996 – the bureaucratic wheels grinding exceeding slowly – Bruce Carpenter, together with Chris Hodges at St John the Divine, had set up a good working structure well before that.

In an interview published in *The Richmond & Twickenham Times* on 10 May

1985 Bruce Carpenter explained his working day:

> I usually start work at 8 am and do not stop until 10pm. There are regular services to give every day with five on Sunday. Then there are articles to be written for the monthly magazine and weekly news sheet.

> I give a lot of talks to different groups in the borough and at school assemblies and on top of this there is all the routine work to be done – writing letters and making phone calls. But I do have one day off a week otherwise I would never see my family.

By 1991, Bruce Carpenter came to feel that he needed a change from parish work (after 32 years) and returned to teaching, as a teaching chaplain to a new Church of England secondary school being established in Ashford, in the Canterbury diocese. This meant he and Angela needed to buy their own house, and Angela also found a teaching post in Ashford. He attended the local parish church in South Ashford, and helped out on a regular basis on Sundays, but, sadly, after three years, the vicar had to leave under a cloud, and he was asked by the Bishop of Maidstone to take on the parish, in order to help the congregation deal with the shock. He did that for a further three years, and then in 1997 he 'retired' at the age of 65.

Bruce was then asked by Canterbury diocese to consider a part-time Warden/Chaplain post in the Rochester diocese, looking after (materially and spiritually) the residents of 36 'Charity' bungalows – a post he held for a further six years. During that time he also studied for a Fine Art degree, part-time at Canterbury College of Art, and then with the Open University.

In 2002 he moved to Southsea, where he helped out in a voluntary capacity for eleven years at Portsmouth Cathedral and, for six years he was Diocesan Mothers' Union Chaplain. Then, in 2013, now sixteen years into his 'retirement', he moved to help out in the parish of St Mary's Portsmouth, which was experiencing a shortage of clergy to minister at its three churches. Now in his eighty seventh year he is still working every Sunday, and still loving it.

Julian Reindorp: 1992–2009

'It is a privilege to be a priest and to be able to both proclaim one's faith and to be with other people on their journey of faith'. Such were the thoughts of Julian Reindorp when interviewed in 2005.

Julian Reindorp was born in 1944 in Durban, South Africa, the eldest of four children. His mother, Alix, was a GP and his father, George, was then a naval chaplain. The family returned to the UK in 1946 when Julian's father – who was subsequently to become Bishop of Guildford (1961–73) and then Bishop of Salisbury (1973–81) - was appointed vicar of St Stephen with St John, Westminster.

Julian Reindorp

Julian first felt the call to ordination whilst at Lancing College, albeit with some trepidation as he was then terrified at the thought of speaking in public – an inhibition which, as those who know him can confirm, he subsequently managed to overcome! For his gap year he returned to South Africa where he learnt about apartheid first hand – 'an important and powerful experience'. Whilst at Trinity College, Cambridge a lifelong interest in issues relating to Christians at work was triggered through a meeting with a group of shop stewards who talked about the role the church could play in the workplace.

For ordination training Julian attended Cuddesdon College in 1967 and, in the following year, the United Theological College, Bangalore. His year in India further broadened his experience, the student body at the College having representatives from 23 denominations and four continents. It also resulted in a thesis, later published as a book, *Leaders and Leadership in the Trade Unions in Bangalore*. Many of the trade union leaders he interviewed were communists, and for the first time Julian had to think about the role of faith not only in work but in politics.

He was ordained curate in 1969, and priest in 1970, and served his curacy in the Poplar Team Ministry (1969–74). In 1974 he became the parish priest in one of the early Local Ecumenical Projects, the Anglican Methodist parish in Chatham of St William Walderslade and St David, Lordswood. Also at this time he was Rochester Diocesan Ecumenical Officer. In 1984 Julian moved on to the then new town of Milton Keynes, becoming team rector there in the Stantonbury Ecumenical Team, serving Anglican, Baptist, Methodist and URC members in a parish of some 50,000 people. Working with colleagues from the four traditions and with people keen to support the growth of both the church and the town, Julian found these years extremely fulfilling.

He became disappointed, however, at the ebbing enthusiasm of the Church of England for Ecumenical Teams and so decided to apply to become team rector at Richmond. He started in January 1992, only five months after Bruce Carpenter had left, and was delighted to inherit the very flexible team constitution that Bruce had set up and the team spirit to go with it.

During his time at Richmond Julian continued to focus on faith at work, running a regular Saturday morning Christians at Work group. In 2000, in obtaining an MA with distinction in Theology and Education from King's College, London, he wrote, and later published, a thesis - *Equipping Christians at Work*. In the diocese he was involved in M.I.L.E. (Mission in London's Economy).

Other approaches to faith explored during Julian's years at Richmond included inter-faith dialogue, group discussion and public debates. Through his colleague Rev. Ruth Scott there was an annual sermon from Rabbi Guy Hall, and preaching from Imam Haleema, one of the few women imams. The team also began both visiting and sharing in dialogue with Kingston Mosque. Julian also instigated a ten week annual course, *Exploring Christianity,* involving people from all three churches; and the outcome of another course, *Encountering God*, was a very professional DVD in which participants explained what faith meant to them. The team also published a book of prayers – *Seeds of Hope – Living Prayer.*

Public debates were held on important international issues, such as the Israel Palestinian situation and the Iraq War, and Julian chaired the Richmond Stop the War group in protest against the Iraq War. He also led two parish trips to the Holy Land.

Julian was at Richmond for eighteen years and is remembered with huge affection by all his friends there. Always cheerful and a special friend to all, he will have covered many thousands of miles on his red Honda 90 as he scootered round the parish, visiting the homes of virtually all his parishioners. And he had an astonishing propensity to remember, without fail, the names of all.

Julian could draw the best out of people. For example, at smaller funerals people could sometimes find themselves, unexpectedly and at Julian's prompting, relating their memories of the departed. And one couple that Julian was due to marry remember he had asked them to do some homework first – each to write down any possible 'pinch points' and what Faith meant to them. Then, rather to their dismay, he instructed them to read out to each other what they had written, something that in fact proved to be immensely helpful to them.

At baptisms Julian had a lovely way of carrying the baby down the aisle during the service, keeping the baby happy with constant movement and the congregation pleased to become involved. It was also the case that Julian kept all his toys at the church – or, at least, so children eager to take home playthings from Junior Church were told – "these are Julian's toys". Nor was he shy of appearing in an Elvis costume, or whatever suited that year's theme, at the May Fair.

Julian 'retired' in 2009 and he and Louise moved to Teddington. He regularly takes services in both the parish of St James, Hampton Hill and another thirty-three parishes either side of the Thames. He also continues to be involved in charity work. He is a patron of the Rainbow Trust, an education charity in Cape Town, a role that is particularly special to him as the charity operates in the area where his mother did her medical training in the 1930s. He is also chair of Hope Outreach UK which carries out missionary work, and funds welfare projects, in Sri Lanka.

Ministers in the 21st century

Robert Titley: 2009–15

Robert Titley was born in Woolwich, South East London, in 1956 as the youngest of three, with two sisters. When he was four the family moved to Orpington, Kent. Sent to Sunday school at the local Methodist church, it was there that he came to faith. Educated at Chislehurst & Sidcup Grammar School and then Christ's College, Cambridge – where he read Classics – Robert joined the National Coal Board in 1978. After some months training, which included time at a colliery in Durham, he worked in the Industrial Relations Department, in the unlikely setting of Belgravia.

In 1981 Robert began training as a Methodist minister at Wesley House, Cambridge, but became 'a victim of ecumenism' when he felt called to ordained ministry in the Church of England. He completed his training at Westcott House, an Anglican theological college literally over the road (Jesus Lane) from Wesley.

Robert Titley

Robert was ordained deacon in 1985 (and priest a year later) and began thirty years' ministry in the Diocese of Southwark. In 1988, after a curacy in Sydenham, he became chaplain at Whitelands College, part of what is now the University of Roehampton. Then in 1994 he became a parish priest in West Dulwich. At the beginning of his time as vicar of All Saints he completed a PhD (on the philosopher and biblical scholar Austin Farrer). In 2000, the halfway point of Robert's ministry, the church of All Saints suffered a major fire and the following six years were dominated by the task of rebuilding. Robert was also rural dean for Streatham for two years until, in 2006, he became Diocesan Director of Ordinands, working with candidates for ordination, a post which also carried a canonry at Southwark Cathedral.

Robert was appointed Team Rector of Richmond in 2010 and during his five years there he was to instigate a major refurbishment programme at St Mary Magdalene. His vision was to enhance the church's historic role as a place of Christian celebration, worship and prayer and also to extend and improve its use by the broader community of Richmond for educational, social and other appropriate cultural and community purposes.

Planning for such a project takes time, with the process of obtaining faculties (consent from the Diocese for building alterations) sometimes being frustratingly and grindingly slow. However, although much of the work was to be completed after Robert had moved on from Richmond in 2015, his legacy was the outline scheme and the momentum to see it through. And the church was blessed to have the financial support of Richmond Church Charity Estates (see p.5) which together with some generous private donations provided all of the funding.

The works carried out at St Mary Magdalene were to transform both the look and the feel of the interior of the church. The gloomy frosted glass of the nave and clerestory windows, which had been installed in 1866, were replaced with mouth-blown clear glass. The church immediately felt a more open and welcoming place. The undistinguished pitch-pine bench-pew seating, another legacy from 1866, was replaced with moveable bench seating, so that the interior space could be used more creatively. Other significant changes were a new floor in Purbeck stone, with underfloor heating, new toilets and kitchen facilities, and the introduction of a new lighting and sound system. The church could face the future with renewed confidence.

Robert also encouraged worshippers to focus upon the liturgy, so that the meaning and significance of all of the services was made clear, particularly for newcomers to the church. New service booklets were provided containing thoughts and explanations on the various services. And in 2011, repeated by popular request in 2012, he ran a fascinating series called The English Eucharist. Held on Wednesday mornings in Lent, the idea was to give people an understanding of how the Communion service had developed in the Church of England over the centuries. The educated Richmond congregation naturally took in their stride the pre-Reformation service, the Mass of Sarum Rite, said in Latin.

Another innovation was the involvement of Richmond Team Ministry in the Street Pastor scheme, providing reassurance, safety and support for people on the streets at night, through listening, caring and helping those in need; Robert was himself an active member of the team. Richmond also benefited from his administrative skills, and it was these that singled him out for his next posting.

In 2015 Robert became Canon Treasurer of Salisbury Cathedral. His duties cover the care of the Cathedral's 'treasures' – its congregation, but also the building and its contents, including a copy of Magna Carta, and the Cathedral's team of masons, glaziers and other craftspeople (there are both men and women).

Robert met Caroline, herself a native of Richmond, when they were students in Cambridge and they were married in 1981. During her twenty-first century Richmond years, Caroline began training for ordination and was ordained in Salisbury Cathedral in 2017. After a career in the housing association movement she became Curate of Wilton, the ancient capital of Wiltshire. They have two grown-up children, James and Julia. Both work in fundraising in the charity sector and, in James' case, by night in a rock band.

Wilma Roest: 2016 –

Reflecting upon her appointment as Team Rector in 2016 Wilma has expressed the view that this was an incredibly brave decision on the part of the Team Ministry, she being both the first woman vicar and a foreigner. If her assessment is correct then, it has to be said, fortune favours the brave.

Wilma was born in Gouda, The Netherlands, the eldest of four children and, with her mother being a foster parent, she is blessed with also having foster brothers and sisters. Her father, now retired, was a headteacher. She was brought up in the Dutch Reformed Church and attended primary and secondary schools in Rotterdam and Vlaardingen. University was Rijksuniversiteit of Utrecht, where Wilma obtained an MA in Musicology in 1988, with a particular interest in Renaissance music. Her final thesis was on the Dutch composer, Johan Wagenaar (1862–1941), whose archive she catalogued at the Dutch Musical Archive in The Hague.

Wilma Roest

Music has always had a central role in Wilma's life, and from her youngest days; there was much music making in the family home. She firmly believes that good music in worship enables people to express their faith beyond words, and to experience with others a shared spirituality. Indeed, it was the choral tradition of the Church of England – on hearing Choral Evensong at Westminster Abbey on her first weekend in the UK in 1988 – that lead Wilma to become an Anglican.

After university Wilma decided to spend some time in London, doing research at the British Library and bringing her English up to scratch. Living in Carshalton Beeches, and working as an au pair, she planned to stay for no more than six months but then, one thing led to another!

Wilma has a natural affinity with children and young people and decided, like her father, to become a teacher. Initially she was at a primary school in Croydon, and then another in Thornton Heath. And it was during these years, in the mid 1990s, that Wilma started to explore her vocation. Women were first ordained as priests in the Church of England in 1994 and one day someone at church asked Wilma whether she had considered ordination. Initially she was rather surprised at this novel idea, but the seed had been sown.

In 1996 Wilma commenced a three-year part-time course at South East Institute of Theological Education, in evenings and at weekends, whilst continuing to teach. She was ordained deacon in 1999, and priest in 2000. She describes how these were sometimes difficult years for women priests, with traditionalists enmeshed in their own prejudices. Once she was spat at on a train, and called Beelzebub. Some refused to receive communion from a woman.

Wilma's first appointment, initially as a curate, was at St. Mary the Virgin, Merton Park. Then, in 1992, she became Team Vicar in the North Lambeth Team, with responsibility for St. Peter's, Vauxhall, a 'pretty challenging' area. In 2006 she moved on, being appointed Vicar of St Mary and St John the Divine, Balham – 'a wonderfully mixed, diverse place to live'. During her ten years at Balham Wilma also became engaged in social issues. She was, for example, chair of Kennington Sure Start serving vulnerable families, chair of Townscape Group, working for a better living and working environment in Balham's town centre, and also actively involved in the Balham Town Centre Partnership, helping to secure a £1.7M grant for town centre improvements. She was Area Dean of Tooting from 2009 to 2016.

And then, in 2016, Wilma was appointed Team Rector and, after more than eight hundred years, Richmond parish had a woman as the minister in charge. Others had paved the way, Richmond having previously had women ministers, all of whom were a full endorsement, if any is needed, of the benefits of ordaining women. And a special word needs to be said of Rev. Ruth Scott, who so sadly died in 2019. Ordained in 1994 – one of the first women to be ordained into the Church of England – Ruth was a woman with 'swashbuckling courage, a mane of strawberry-blond hair and an honesty that was invariably disarming' (as her obituary in *The Times* so neatly put it).

The first thing many people say, when asked what strikes them most about Wilma, is 'her wonderful voice'. Both her singing voice – 'when I first heard it within the morning service tingles ran down my neck' - and the clarity of her speaking voice, itself the outward expression of clarity of thought. Others refer to her great affinity to children and her ability to include them in the act of worship. Some note with enjoyment that Wilma's skills as an infant school teacher have never left her, as she invites the congregation to have a second go if they give an underwhelming response! And then there is that special moment of eye contact as she delivers the host to a communicant.

Wilma also brings to her role both organisational skills and practicality. The major construction works at St Mary Magdalene were to get underway within a year of her arrival and, whilst many other churches would have closed during this time, the congregation were treated to exploring new spaces and aspects within the church. As regards the works, Wilma's attention to detail was very apparent, both on utilitarian issues and especially on liturgical designs. And she needed only one look at the rooms within St Mary Magdalene, on her arrival, before a clear out was required, a skip hired for the purpose.

Wilma also has a facility for reaching out beyond the immediate congregation. For example, in 2019 the members of The Richmond Society were treated to a fascinating evening talk about both her life and St Mary Magdalene. And, very specially, on Ash Wednesday Wilma goes out into the town giving ashes (ceremoniously making a cross on the forehead) to those passers-by and rough sleepers who wish it.

Wilma often recalls the pleasure she felt when watching the stonemason cutting her name into the stone tablet by the West door, adding it to the list of ministers' names stretching back to 1541. And no doubt, for his part, the stonemason carved her name with pride.

Further reading

Casaubon, Edward, 'All actors are knaves and all actresses harlots': Richmond clergy and the theatre, (*Richmond History*, No 34, 2013)

Cloake, John, *Cottages and Common Fields of Richmond and Kew* (Phillimore, 2001)

Cloake, John, Curates and Ministers of Richmond Parish Church before 1660 (*Richmond History*, No 14, 1993)

Cloake, John, In Search of the Vicarage: The Many Homes of the Richmond Parish Clergy (*Richmond History*, No 7, 1986)

Cloake, John, *Richmond Past* (Historical Publications Ltd, 1991)

Cloake, John, *Royal Bounty: The Richmond Parish Lands Charity* 1786–1991 (Richmond Parish Lands Charity, 1992)

Cloake, John – The Pulpit in Richmond Parish Church, (*Richmond History*, No 10, 1989)

Kendall, The Rev. J.F. – *A Short History of the Church of England* (A. & C. Black, 1914)

Hiscoke & Son, *Richmond Notes* (a monthly magazine) March 1863–September 1868, (Hiscoke & Son, Richmond)

Hoare, Edward, ed. by Rev. J. H. Townsend, *A Record of his Life based upon a Brief Biography* (Hodder & Stoughton, 1896)

Jones, Anthea, *A Thousand Years of the English Parish*, (Cassell Paperbacks, Cassell & Co. (2000))

Lysons, Rev. Daniel, *The Environs of London, Vol. 1, the County of Surrey*, (T. Cadell, London, 1792)

Manning, Rev. Owen, and Bray, William, *The History and Antiquities of the County of Surrey,* White, Cochrane, London, 1804–14)

Piper, A. Cecil, *A History of the Parish Church of St Mary Magdalene, Richmond, Surrey* (London, 1947)

Pounds, N.J.G., *A History of the English Parish*, (Cambridge University Press, 2000)

Treadwell, Michael, Swift, Richard Coleire, and the Origins of Gulliver's Travels (*The Review of English Studies*, Volume XXXIV, Issue 135, August 1983, pp. 304–11)

Wodehouse, P.G. – *The Great Sermon Handicap*, (Hodder & Stoughton, 1933)

Although every effort has been taken to ensure that everything in this book is factually correct, it is not intended to be an academic work, so the text has not been weighed down with notes referencing the sources from which information has been obtained. However, a full record of source material will be deposited with the Richmond Local Studies Library and Archive.

List of Illustrations

© Alamy
Illustration of a 17th century minister: Richard Baxter, 1615–91, English Puritan church leader, theologian and controversialist
Illustration of an 18th century minister: Richard Watson, 1737–1816, Bishop of Llandaff

© Jackie Baines Studio
Plan: Homes of the Vicars

Bridgeman Images
Portrait of Guido Ferdinando Tenducci, by Thomas Gainsborough, about 1773. The Barber Institute of Fine Arts; *Gulliver awakening in Lilliput,* by Arthur Rackham. De Agostini Picture Library

By courtesy of the estate of John Cloake
Glebe House, photograph 1965

© Collage – The London Picture Archive
The Georgian South Aisle in 1797, by James Peller Malcolm
St Mary Magdalene, March 28 1807

© Fitzwilliam Museum, Cambridge
Gilbert Wakefield, Margaret Wakefield, Thomas Wakefield, sketches by John Downman, 1778

The Huntington Library, San Marino, California
A detail from p. 142 of Abiel Borfet's copy of the works of Benjamin Jonson, 1616

Photo © National Gallery of Ireland
Nicholas Brady, c. 1715, attributed to Hugh Howard

© National Portrait Gallery
James Thomson, after John Patoun, circa 1746; Francis Hughes-Hallett, by Carlo Pellegrini, published in *Vanity Fair*, 18 December 1886

By courtesy of John Oates
John Oates upon an elephant; Margaret Thatcher, attending a memorial service at St Bride's, with Canon Oates

By courtesy of the Parochial Church Council of Richmond, St Mary Magdalene with St Matthias and St John the Divine
Harry Dupuis, Max Binney, John Kendall, George Gray, Montague Barlow, Derek Landreth, John Oates, Bruce Carpenter, Julian Reindorp, Robert Titley, Wilma Roest, photograph portraits; All Saints chapel window

By courtesy of Louise Reindorp
Canon Reindorp on his red Honda 90

Richmond upon Thames Local Studies Library and Archive
Charles Procter, photograph, 1878; 20 Pounds Reward, Handbill, 1874; National Schools Richmond, S.E View; an 1851 depiction of a baptism in the church.

By courtesy of Alexandra Robb
Photographs of the pulpit and a medallion

By courtesy of Derek Robinson
A curate preaching to the text of Genesis 1:3, by Alexandra Robb